THE ALL

MANIFESTING REALITY

DEREK PEW

The All: Manifesting Reality

Derek Pew

Published by Derek Pew, 2024.

THE ALL: MANIFESTING REALITY

First edition. August 12, 2024.

Copyright © 2024 Derek Pew.

ISBN: 979-8227126085

Written by Derek Pew.

Table of Contents

THE ALL

Manifesting Reality

Introduction

This book was channeled to me through meditation.

I am not a guru or a mystic or a medical doctor.

I am an entrepreneur, philanthropist and business leader who was using a meditation practice to move away from self-imposed doubts, fears, and limitations in running my businesses and I received what I have written here.

It is applicable to everyone.

If you are like me, you envision your life as having some measure of success and happiness, but it is not always obvious how to get there.

Many times, it feels as if our work is futile, or life happens by chance. We tend not to believe that we are in control of our own reality.

Here, I am providing you a way forward if you are feeling like you are trapped in a cycle of doubts, limiting beliefs, feel like life is not in your control, feel lost, disconnected, unlucky, victimized, scared, angry, or fearful. I will show you things that have been shown to me.

These things are all hidden like many great secrets "in plain sight" and are, at the same time, the most familiar things to us and the things we find hardest to believe.

There is a way to live our life to our greatest potential and to take control of our life choices, our success and happiness, and even find bliss.

It is a process, and a practice that we will explore in Part 2 of this book, that takes us back to our most natural existence and to intentional control of our reality.

Before we begin, certain terms that are used in this book are used in many contexts outside this book, and I want to define them for you in the way that I am using them.

The All, after which this book is titled, is the infinite. The All is everything including the All.

When I speak of our soul in this book, I am not making a religious reference. I am instead speaking of our integration into everything, our common tie to everything else in the All and the All itself.

Because it is connected to everything else in the All and the All itself, our soul is both unique to us and not unique to us. It has knowledge that seems magical or supernatural because that knowledge does not relate to our experience as biological humans.

Our consciousness as biological humans is our pathway to our soul and, therefore, to everything in the All and the All itself.

Our consciousness serves as our mind's context and the thoughts that our minds generate both passively from information received by our senses and intentionally. Both of those are equally real.

When I talk about the "intuition of our soul" in this book, I am talking about the conscious knowledge that we have through our soul's integration into everything in the All and the All itself.

By listening to the intuition of our soul, we can predict, manifest, and create in ways that seem supernatural, but are natural because of our natural connection to everything in the All and the All itself.

Because of how we evolved and the nature of our existence, our biological minds fill us with thoughts that limit and often prohibit our ability to recognize that we control our own reality.

These thoughts also limit our ability to find our way to our soul, the intuitive knowledge it posesses and the power of the energies and planes of existence where it resides, because none of that is relatable to our biological experience.

It is therefore important for us to understand where the sources of our limitations come from so that we can uproot them and live life to our fullest potential.

In Part 1 we will develop an analytic understanding of the sources of our doubts, fears and limitations that prevent us from being our total selves.

In Part 2, we work together to reverse engineer those limitations and find our way back to taking control of our reality, listening to the intuition of our soul, connecting to broader reality, and manifesting the supernatural.

Our reality is not what we think it is, and we hold the power to determine the trajectory of our lives.

I am going to challenge what you believe, expose the limitations of your reality, open your mind to what is truly real, and give you the tools to achieve everything that is possible for you to achieve in this life.

This book contains a large amount of information in a relatively small number of words.

Unlike other books, each sentence may require its own breath.

Please read what follows at a pace that allows you to digest what is written. Many of the topics are complex and may be unfamiliar.

If a concept is too complex, move past it and come back to it after you have completed the book.

For some chapters I have included summaries as helpful guides, not as replacements to the chapters. For other chapters I have not included summaries because they do not lend themselves to summary.

I frequently cite other books and authors and encourage you to read those books as they provide broader insight into what is here if the topics of those books interest you.

At the end of this book is a bibliography for easy reference of all the books cited herein.

PART 1
Chapter 1

Reality and Mentalism

At the beginning of the 20th Century, a mysterious book was published called "*The Kybalion: A Study of the Hermetic Philosophy of Ancient Egypt and Greece*," written by a mystery author or authors calling himself or themselves The Three Initiates.

The book describes the principles of the universe and claims to be the source of all modern religions.

The book derives from the teachings of an ancient philosopher, referred to as the greatest of the greats, Hermes Trismegistus, who understood the reality and principles of the universe. Hermes Trismegistus either became the basis for the Greek god Hermes and the Egyptian god Thoth or was derived from the knowledge base that formed around them.

Hermes Trismegistus' teachings are also the basis of Western occult beliefs, mystical, magical and supernatural belief systems, alchemy, and the teachings of many secret societies.

I find the teachings of the Kybalion to be incredibly consistent with the revelations I have had in my meditation practice as they relate to the nature of the context of the All.

Briefly, the Kybalion sets forth seven core principles of the context of the All: mentalism, correspondence, vibration, polarity, rhythm, cause and effect and gender.

Don't worry about most of these principles yet, as we will discuss them later in the book in more depth. But think about them generally and keep them in the back of your mind as you read on.

The most important principle of the context of the All is that everything that exists, including the All, exists in the mentalism of the All.

That is to say that the All is mind, and the universe is mental.

Let's explore what I mean by "mind" and "mentalism," because we use those words every day in ways that can make their usage here confusing.

The universe that we know originated from the All and is part of the All, therefore, the All is both the context for and the manifestation of our universe.

By context I mean that our universe emerged from something. That something I describe as context because a context is the circumstances that form the setting for an event. In our case, the event was the manifestation of our universe.

We have insight into the construct of the All as both context and manifestation in ourselves.

Our consciousness is the circumstances that form the setting for our thoughts.

Our consciousness provides for our creation of new thoughts, their modification, there interaction with other thoughts, but our consciousness itself is not thought. It is the context from which our thoughts manifest.

Just like the All, our consciousness does not require time or space, but our thoughts do.

This is why I say the All is "mind." Like our consciousness, the All is comprised of both its contextual medium and everything it manifests, just like our mind is comprised of the context of our consciousness and all the thoughts it manifests.

Keep this construct in mind as we move on in this book and recognize that reality is not just the things, or what scientists call "quanta," in our universe but the context that manifest those quanta as well.

We experience the quanta in our universe with our senses.

As biological humans most of our daily manifestations derive passively from our senses because our senses are critical to our continued biological existence. The result is that we live under a powerful and fundamental misconception that only what we sense with our senses is real.

But our senses did not evolve to define our reality. Our senses evolved to keep us alive. Our passive manifestations from our senses do not define what is real. In fact, what we manifest from our mind-sense interaction has little to do with the true reality of the universe we interact with and nothing to do with the context that manifested our universe.

For example, we accept the existence of a chair because when we sit down on it, we sense its existence holding us up. The chair is "real" to us because we "feel" it.

But as we will discuss in Part 1, when we experience something through our senses, the experience is a manifestation of our minds.

Everything about the chair, how it looks, how it feels, how we perceive it, even our emotions about it are manifested by our minds.

Yes, the chair exists, but our manifestation of the chair is unique to us. If our senses had evolved differently, the chair would still exist, but we would manifest it differently.

The existence of a chair would have a different reality to us.

As we will discuss later, the chair is an amalgamation of quanta we call atoms, just like we are, and even smaller quanta that make up the atoms.

The interaction between our atoms and the chair's atoms we manifest as physical touch even if what we are sensing is the interaction of forces that derive from the existence of the quanta that make up atoms.

As biological humans, we are mind, and we are mental. Our reality is entirely of our creation. There is no distinction between what we passively manifest from our senses and what we intentionally manifest from the intuition of our souls.

Just like the All, we magically create quanta, in our case, thoughts, out of a context.

I was explaining this concept of manifestation to a friend when we were stopped in a car at a traffic light.

I asked my friend what she saw when she looked at the traffic light.

She said, "I see a red light."

I told her that the red light was a manifestation of her mind, and that all that was there was a machine that emitted photons of certain wavelengths that her mind manifested as either red, yellow or green.

I told her that colors do not exist without her sensory-organ-mind connection, in this case her retina and her mind. The photons emitted by the traffic light have a wavelength, but manifesting color from that wavelength is entirely a manifestation of her mind.

It would be as if I told her to remember that the number 2 is always blue. The number 2 has no inherent color, but she would manifest blue with 2 based on my directive.

She looked at me like I had lost my mind because it is so hard for us to move past our manifested, sensory-based reality. That manifestation is what helps keep us alive and is powerful.

The reality of the traffic light is one thing and the reality that we manifest about the traffic light is something different.

Yet we believe that the reality of the traffic light is what we manifest about it, and not what it is. Just like the sofa.

This is an important distinction because the reality that we manifest for ourselves is what we live in.

We create realties that do not exist without us.

As sentient beings, we have a unique connection to the All because our consciousness provides a context for thought manifestation.

Our mentalism, our consciousness, is therefore what reveals to us as biological humans the nature of the All.

To understand the nature of the All we must look inward to our own thought manifestation and our own consciousness. From this exercise we begin to understand reality.

But first we must acknowledge that what we believe is reality is not reality at all.

Let's begin with our known universe, one manifestation of the All.

The total manifest quanta of our universe in The All I represent as a pure circle.

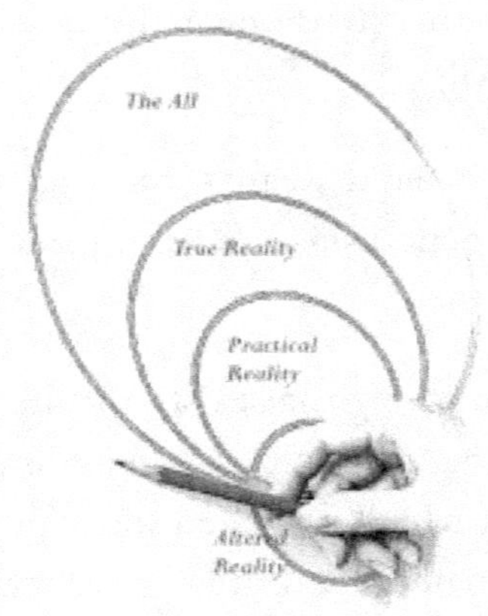

I will frequently refer to the pure circle of the All in this book to define all the manifested quanta of the All without the manifestations of our and other sentient beings' mentalism.

The limited subset of the All that constitutes this Earth Life System, all the quanta that exist within our existence, I call our True Reality.

What we are capable of perceiving and understanding with our senses and our biological mind is yet a smaller subset of our True Reality which I call our Practical Reality. Practical Reality is our biological experience of our True Reality through our senses.

Finally, what generates our daily thoughts, our mentalism, our reality, is an even smaller and altered subset of our Practical Reality which I call our Altered Reality.

Altered Reality is the reality created by our thoughts that do not derive from our consciousness. Altered Reality includes true and untrue things, but all of it is an extension of the quanta that make up the manifestations of the All.

In the above graphic, Altered Reality, the reality created by our and other sentient beings' mentalism, extends outside the pure circle of the All.

Importantly, while everything that exists within the pure circle of the All is true, meaning that it exists without human or other sentient beings' mentalism, that which is created solely by our mentalism is not necessarily true, but equally as real and is graphically represented by the portion of our Altered Reality that extends beyond the pure circle of the All.

I may believe that the world is flat, and for as long as I live in that reality, I have created it as part of the Altered Reality that extends beyond the pure circle of the All, but it is untrue.

Each reality is a limited subset of the quanta manifest of the All.

We will start with the quanta manifest of the All (excluding the existence of sentient beings), and then will peel back the layers of the onion of our reality down to our Altered Reality to analytically show ourselves how limiting our day-to-day thoughts of reality are in this Earth life system.

To find our way to our integration into the All and the reality that is derived from its context, we need to first acknowledge and believe that our reality is a manifestation that deceives us into believing that what is real is our Altered Reality.

Without that acknowledgement, our mind in our Altered Reality will lead us to deny that any other reality exists, and we will remain trapped.

Where our Altered Reality ends and all other reality begins is where we start to get in touch with the supernatural abilities that taking control of our reality and intentionally manifesting from the intuition that our soul provides.

People say we die alone in this Earth life system as biological humans. But we live alone in this system as well because every aspect of our reality while we are alive in this life system is based on our own internal mentalism.

While this may sound scary, it is empowering because it means that we are each empowered to determine our own reality, but until now we have mostly done that in a passive way developed through neurological processes determined by evolution.

Outside this Earth life system, we are never alone. We are connected to the quanta and context of the All. We are as un-alone as imaginably possible and that is the natural existence of our consciousness.

Let's more expansively begin to understand the limitations of our True Reality.

Science

Science exists as a way for us as biological humans to explain our True Reality.

To do that, science looks at what we can sense or measure in our True Reality and then builds theories and models to define the nature and predict the behavior of the quanta in our True Reality. It does that by dividing quanta into fields or particles, energy or mass.

It is important to understand that science does not exist to define reality. Science exists to explain our universe. In that way, it is much the same as our senses – practically important to us but not where we learn about reality.

Physics derives from ancient philosophical concepts of True Reality and has been enormously successful at predicting the behaviors and relationships of quanta.

Quanta are the particles and energies that make up our universe.

But by focusing on the quanta, physics reaffirms our bias to believe that reality is made up of what we can sense, when reality is so much greater than that.

Let's further understand how True Reality and our Altered Reality differ by further discussing light.

Remember the traffic light?

Light does not exist without us and other sentient beings that depend on sight from an interaction with photons.

Our minds manifest light from the interaction of photons hitting our retinas, and without the reality of light created by us and other organisms that create the thought of light, it would not exist in the All.

We experience photons every day in our True Reality but have no idea what a photon is because our minds manifest photons as light and color, not as photons.

But a photon exists as a quantum of the All separate from our manifestation of light and color. This illustrates how the pure circle of the All is different from our Altered Reality and how our Altered Reality distances us from knowing the All.

We can describe the behavior of a photon using mathematical equations derived from Wave-Particle Duality theory provided to us by physics.

Because quanta in our universe exist as either mass or energy or some combination of both, physics uses two mathematical theories to describe everything in our universe.

One theory describes quanta when it is energy using wave theory. The other theory describes quanta when it is mass using particle theory. The combination of these theories is called Wave-Particle Duality Theory.

We can replicate experiments testing the validity of Wave-Particle Duality theory and prove to ourselves that it is a good predictor of photon behavior in True Reality.

But the theory doesn't describe what a photon is in True Reality. It merely defines the parameters of and predicts the behavior of a photon in relation to other quanta.

We don't have anything that we encounter in our Altered Reality that we can relate a photon to even though we experience photons every day because our experience with photons is a manifestation that results from our evolution as biological beings.

A photon is not like a banana or a rock or even a wave or a particle. It is unlike anything in our lives other than itself. It is supernatural and yet it is a critical part of our daily lives.

Even physicists refer to photons as "light," and the speed at which they move their information as the "speed of light," demonstrating how our own manifestations make it into our description of True Reality.

Nevertheless, science exposes to us the limitations that we face in existing in our True Reality in understanding the reality of the All.

Even if our Altered Reality was the same as our True Reality, our ability to understand the reality of the All would be limited.

Obvious Matter

In this Earth life system, we developed in a portion of the quanta of the All that is made up entirely of quanta that physicists call "obvious matter."

A bus, a lasagna, a flower, a raindrop, are all obvious matter. All the quanta that make up those things are also obvious matter and constitute the basis of what we think of as nearly all our True Reality.

We live in an obvious matter house or apartment, eat obvious matter food, drink obvious matter beverages, wear obvious matter clothes and scratch our obvious matter heads.

However, physicists have discovered through observation and experimentation that some other form of quanta must exist in the All and that the obvious matter that makes up our experience represents only about fifteen percent of the quanta of the All.

The remaining roughly eighty-five percent of the quanta of the All, physicists refer to as "dark" matter, as the astrophysicist and Harvard professor Dr. Lisa Randall describes in her book "*Dark Matter and the Dinosaurs.*"

Dr. Randall explains that while we have no experience with dark matter directly, without dark matter we would not exist, and neither would have the dinosaurs. And the demise of the dinosaurs, that cataclysmic meteor, would not exist either.

Dark matter is something we can't see, but we theorize exists because of its effect on other quanta.

There is no dark matter in our True Reality, so there is nothing for us to relate it to. Dark matter is supernatural.

It's like the photon, except that we manifest the photon as light and color.

We don't experience dark matter at all except that we experience the cause and effects of its theoretical existence.

We can only comprehend dark matter as a predictive abstraction, and as a predictive abstraction, 85% of the quanta derived from the context of the All becomes part of our mentalism, part of our Altered Reality.

Dimensions and Time

We also developed in a part of the All limited at least in terms of our True Reality to three physical dimensions and time.

As Dr. Randall points out in her book *"Warped Passages: Unraveling the Mysteries of the Universe's Hidden Dimensions,"* that mathematics predicts that there could be an infinite number of dimensions of nearly any size in an infinite number of universes, and time, and our limited three other dimensions may or may not be relevant to the reality of the All.

We drive down the street in our three-dimensional car in our three-dimensional bodies and, as we do so, time passes.

Because energies, energy fields and planes of existence exist everywhere in the quanta of the All, the fact that our True Reality is different than most of the reality of the All is an important starting point in understanding that our True, Practical, and Altered realities are fundamentally limited compared to the reality of the All.

To illustrate the dimensional limitations of our True Reality, try to imagine what it would be like to encounter something consisting of more than three dimensions and time in our world.

We can't. It is an abstraction because there is nothing in our Altered Reality to relate that to.

So, let's do something easier.

We can relate to two dimensions since two dimensional things exist in our three-dimensional world - a comic strip, for example, is a two-dimensional world for the characters in the comic strip.

Let's imagine ourselves in that comic strip world to understand how odd interaction with a larger dimensional world would be.

A three-dimensional sphere entering our two-dimensional world would appear out of nowhere as a point, expand into a growing circle then shrink back to a point and disappear.

It would be very hard for our minds that developed in a two-dimensional world to understand or explain using the science of our two-dimensional world.

Yet, in our three physical dimension world, we try to explain the All from the perspective of our three physical dimensions and time. It is the best we can do without abstraction.

It is no more valid than a two physical dimension world trying to explain our three physical dimension world in the context of two dimensions.

Maybe the existence of other dimensions could explain, for example, our encounters with other life systems like UFOs and how they are able to appear and disappear and move in ways that do not conform with the rules that govern our true reality.

If a UFO were tubular in a fourth dimension and entered our three dimensions at an angle it would look to us as a spherical object that appeared, moved quickly along a linear path only to disappear again.

Whether other dimensions explain UFOs or not, there is no reason for us to limit how we look at our existence in the limitation of our four dimensions.

But it is critical for us to accept that our three physical dimensions and time are only a limited reality of the All.

Three physical dimensions and time are a core part of our True Reality, but they are only part of the mentalism of the All.

Summary

Science has shown us that our True Reality is limited not only because it is made up entirely of obvious matter but also because there is no reason to think that the reality of the All is bound by three physical dimensions or time.

The most we can relate to in our human biology is something substantially different from much of the reality of the All in almost every way because of where we exist in the quanta of the All.

Yet we make decisions on what is real and what is faith, based on a reality that we have already demonstrated to be a very limited reality.

That is only the beginning in unwinding the limitations that are imposed on us by our Altered Reality and we need to unwind all of them to cognitively take control of our reality, reconnect with our soul and live life to our fullest potential.

Chapter 2

Practical Reality

As biological humans, our human form evolved over hundreds of thousands of years in ways that maximized our survival as an organism, not our survival at a cellular or atomic level, nor our connection to the All.

It was practically important for us to identify obvious matter like a spear flying at us, instead of radio waves, X-rays, Gamma rays or other things that primarily only affect us at an atomic level, fly right through us but do not generally lead to our demise, at least not immediately.

It is not practically important to us as biological humans if one of our atoms loses an electron, but a bus careening towards us on the street is obvious matter that poses great threat to our obvious matter body and our survival.

It doesn't matter for our survival that the True Reality of we and the bus is that we are made up of tiny things that we describe using particle theories and wave theories many of which carry charges of plus and minus, and between them there is a lot of space, or that at a very tiny level, everything we are, is just a lot of open space and energy.

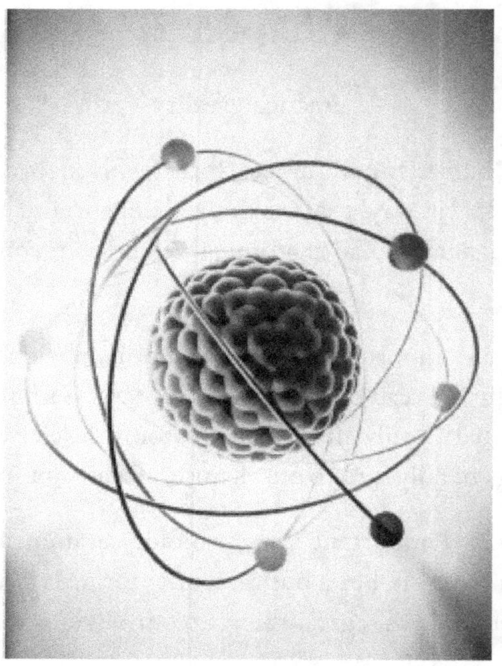

These tiny, charged particles that make us up, and the space between them, come from and exist in energy fields in which everything exists, among them the weak force which is the force that holds our atoms together and without which we would not exist, the strong force which holds subatomic particles together without which we would not exist, and the Higgs Field, also without which we would not exist.

Without these forces we would not be able to sit on a chair and, in that way, we manifest them as the feeling of solid matter. But we view that "solidness" as reality when the "solidness" is just a manifestation of our mind of the aggregation of these forces.

The Higgs Field and Higgs Boson

While we have known about the other forces for a while, the Higgs Field is a relatively new physics discovery that solves problems with certain predictive theories of physics.

The Higgs Field does some amazing and even magical things. It exists everywhere in the All and carries an infinite amount of the energy that keeps atoms together and is responsible for, among other things, creating mass and ensuring that the weak force that holds atoms together only exists in very tiny spaces.

Like the photon, which is the boson of the electromagnetic field, the Higgs Boson is the communication particle of the Higgs Field and because it can do things like deliver energy or mass from what appears to us as nothing, it has been called the God particle.

Maybe the Higgs Field is our manifestation of the contextual nature of the All or the bridge between the contextual nature of the All and its manifestations.

Gravity

We also experience gravity in our True Reality. We experience gravity because we stick to the Earth's surface instead of flying off it, but we can't define gravity.

Einstein told us that gravity is a warping of the time space continuum based on the mass of an object.

You can imagine this by imagining a rubber sheet onto which you place a ball in the middle, the rubber sheet will sag at the point of the ball creating a warping of the sheet based on the ball's mass.

The rubber sheet represents the time-space continuum.

If you stand on the end of the sheet, you will slide towards the ball because of the warping of time space.

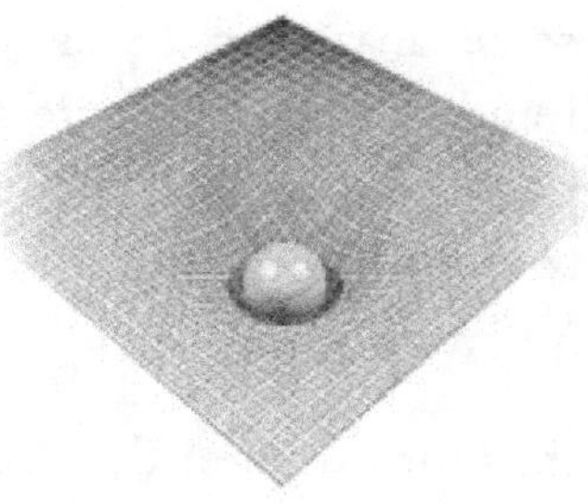

Like a photon, we experience gravity every day when we stand from a seated position, jump, run or walk. It takes energy for us to fight the force of gravity.

While we experience it as a force constantly pulling at us, we only understand it as an abstraction because it is a force that we cannot replicate ourselves in a way that we can sense.

The Weak and Strong Forces

We sense with our senses the weak force and the strong force as "solidness," but the weak force is so powerful that we use it to create heat for nuclear power plants and for the destructive force of nuclear weapons.

The tiny, charged particles that comprise us, are held together by these forces. They vibrate and move in ways we do not feel. They pass through and interact with the Higgs Field and other fields in different ways based on their mass that we cannot sense or fully understand.

They are, at scales, impacted by the bending of time space that we call gravity.

They are us and they are our True Reality. But we do not define ourselves in terms of them.

Our True Reality, therefore, is not something that we can sense.

We only sense what matters to our practical survival.

If we could see at the scale of an atom, we wouldn't be able to identify practical danger.

So instead of our True Reality, we have developed to only sense our Practical Reality.

Now are you beginning to see that what is "real" for us are things that we don't ever think about and the things that we think are real are just manifestations of our minds of our True Reality, which is only a subset of the reality derived from the context of the All?

Summary

To take control of our reality and connect to the energies and energy fields and other planes of existence that exist as quanta of the All, we must first acknowledge the limitations of our True Reality and then realize how much more limited our Practical and Altered Realities are.

The thoughts, fears and worries that arise from our Altered Reality dominate our everyday lives, make us disbelieve that we can control our reality and limit our ability to connect to the intuition of our soul.

These thoughts feel like our reality, but they are not. They are manifestations of our minds of True Reality and become part of the mentalism of the All through our existence.

Chapter 3

The Modifications of Our Practical Reality Caused by Our Senses

We primarily experience our Practical Reality through our senses, and, therefore, our Practical Reality is inherently altered by the biological nature of our senses.

Because we manifest reality through our senses, what we think of as "real" is determined by how we evolved, not by the reality derived from the context of the All.

It is a critical step to accept that everything about our reality is formed by how our mind-sensory function evolved.

Any change in the biological evolution of our senses would alter our reality.

The biological senses we evolved include sight, touch, hearing, taste, and smell. They evolved in ways that decided on how the senses would function.

For instance, we could see in any number of ways. Photon reception is merely how we evolved as did all sentient creatures with eyes.

Our senses developed to support our survival like they did for other living organisms in this Earth life system, and we will refer to all these organisms as "us."

Together these senses make up most of the stimuli that goes into our minds and form the basis of our thoughts.

Survival and sensing True Reality are not necessarily consistent.

As discussed, in this Earth life system we exist in our Practical Reality, in three physical dimensions and time where everything we experience is obvious matter and we can only understand it in a non-abstract way in the context of the information our senses deliver to us and the way our minds manifest reality out of those sense interactions.

We confuse ourselves by thinking that what we sense is real and what we cannot sense is not real or, at minimum, an abstract reality.

Vision

Let's start with vision since we have previously discussed photons.

For those of us who are not blind, a significant amount of the information we take in every day and the thoughts that we derive from our senses come from sight.

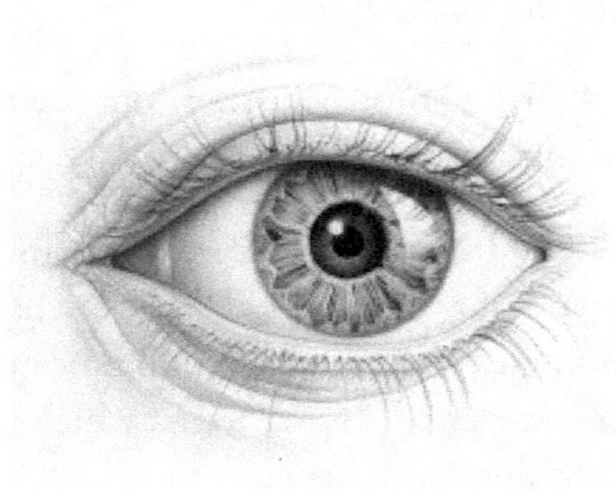

Forces and force fields of the All are constantly communicating using particles to carry those communications. Each force or force field uses a different particle as its communication medium.

Science calls force, or energy, communicating particles bosons.

They are different than, but interact with, the particles that make up obvious matter that are called fermions.

We don't currently know what makes up most of the universe that is dark matter, because we can't see dark matter.

If we sensed things in the All using something other than photons, we might constantly experience and "see" dark matter. Our thoughts would contribute to a different mentalism of the All.

The electromagnetic force's communication particle is the photon.

In our corner of the universe, the photon is the fastest communications particle, and it bounces off obvious matter at differing wavelengths meaning that not only does it tell us that the matter is there, but it gives us some information about the matter.

Sight is provided by photons hitting our retina which then communicates that information to our brain.

As Deepak Chopra and Menas Kafatos explain in their book "*You Are the Universe*," and as we have previously discussed, photons are not inherently luminous, they merely communicate information by delivering a certain wavelength to our retina which then delivers that information to our minds.

Our minds receive the information of photons hitting our retina and manifest it into light and color.

Chopra and Kafatos offer that all reality is manifested by our mentalism. But I would take that further and say that all reality is manifested of the contextual nature of the All and we are a part of that.

Altered Reality extends beyond the pure circle of the All, expanding the mentalism of the All with the creations of our mentalism.

Our Altered Reality that extends beyond the pure circle of the All graphically represents that part of our manifested reality that shares no connection with the remainder of the All.

That part of our Altered Reality makes the remainder of the All supernatural to us and limits our ability to connect with the All because of our inability to relate to it.

We must shed many of those parts of our Altered Reality that lie outside the pure circle of the All, to take control of our reality and connect to our souls.

Unfortunately, most of us live almost exclusively in that part of Altered Reality that lies outside the pure circle of the All, completely disconnected from the remainder of the All.

As we have previously discussed, colors do not exist except in our retina-brain relationship, and our mentalism is what creates light and color in the All. Light and color are not true.

We evolved to manifest color because it is helpful to survival.

We associate different colors with different things. Clear blue water suggests freshness or potability. Green suggests edible vegetation.

Orange, red and yellow suggest fruits and nutritious vitamins, minerals and energy.

Colors can also suggest danger, like the orange and black stripes of a tiger.

A beautiful sunset or sunrise, a beautiful clear Caribbean Sea are not inherently beautiful at all.

They just are.

Our minds manifest beauty because of how we manifest colors.

Visual beauty does not exist except in the relationship between our retinas and our minds.

By selecting the photon as one of our primary sources to receive information about the world around us, we have gained all the benefits of that choice as well as the limitations.

Our ability to sense anything by sight means that we are limited to only observing things that interact with photons and are the same size or larger than the size of a photon, because photons are all we can see.

As a practical matter, our retina brain connection has developed in a way that only allows us to see what is practically important to survival and that is about a tenth of a millimeter of obvious matter which is substantially larger than the size of a photon.

Photons bounce nicely off buses careening towards us and because the photon communicates the information of that bus faster than any other source of information in our true reality that we can sense in our corner of the universe, using photons as our primary sensory communications particle gives us a better chance for survival.

Not only does the photon tell us the bus is coming, when it hits the bus, the bus only reflects certain wavelengths, so we not only know that it is a bus, but that it is yellow with black writing that says "SCHOOL BUS" that gives us even more information about the bus and its contents.

Our minds through our senses similarly manifest a reality that without our sensory system-brain connection would not exist.

Taste and Smell

A chemical compound that contains twelve atoms of carbon, twenty-two atoms of hydrogen and eleven atoms of oxygen is not sweet without our mentalism.

This is the chemical composition of white sugar, and sweetness is a manifestation of our minds.

The fact that it tastes sweet to us is a function of our taste buds, olfactory senses and mind interacting. Sweetness only exists in the mentalism of the All because of us.

Some chemical compounds are important to our biological needs and our brain-sensory organ connection evolved to create a reality of sweetness and pleasure from sweetness that makes us seek out these compounds.

By ingesting them we support our survival.

Similarly, the compound that contains one atom of sodium and one atom of chloride is not salty, but we create the reality of salt in our brains because our biological bodies need these chemicals.

Saltiness only exists in the mentalism of the All because we manifest it.

We get pleasure from tasting salt when we need sodium and chloride.

These atoms interact with our cells to retain water on a hot day and for many other biological functions that help us survive.

Similarly, we manifest different smells associated with different chemicals that enter our nose.

Without our mind-nose connection there are no smells in the All.

Smell, like taste, helps us survive. We can smell if a food is good or bad. We can smell an enemy approaching.

Hearing

Hearing is among the most mysterious of our brain-sensory created realities.

Hearing is the result of receiving the movement of obvious matter in our eardrums.

We call that movement of obvious matter, soundwaves.

Like photons, soundwaves have wavelengths, but like photons which without us are not luminous and do not have color, soundwaves without us don't have pitch or volume.

Calling them soundwaves is a misnomer, because they are just waves of very small obvious matter caused by the collision of obvious matter into other obvious matter.

They do not make any sound except in the context of our mind-sensory organ connection.

We manifest sound and pitch.

As we have learned earlier, one of the principles of the All is that of vibration. Our experience of vibration is a direct connection to the nature of the All.

Both photons and soundwaves are representations of a fundamental state of the All that we receive through sensory organs.

When someone says that a musical note is associated with a particular number of vibrations per second, the note is a manifestation of our mind-eardrum connection.

A note is not a reality that exists outside our mind-sensory organ biology.

But like sight, we manifest beauty and emotion by receiving vibrations.

That beauty or emotion is not objectively present in a collection of wave forms whether from photons or from sound waves.

Followers of sacred geometry suggest that there is a correlation between pleasant sounds and geometry that is an inherent part of this Earthly life system.

Sacred geometry ascribes sacred and symbolic meaning to certain geometric shapes and certain geometric proportions.

Pursuant to sacred geometry, if you add the interior angles of basic shapes – triangle, square, pentagon, hexagon, etc. - and convert the sum of the interior angles of those shapes to hertz or cycles per second the result is the notes that make up perfect major chords.

We manifest major chords as happy.

We manifest slight modifications to those major chords, converting them to minor chords, as sad.

It is, therefore, because of us that beauty and discordance, happiness and sadness associated with waves, exist in the mentalism of the All.

The manifestation of pitch is important to us for many reasons because through the Doppler Effect, where pitch increases as a sound making body approaches and where pitch declines as that same body recedes, we can tell if an object is approaching us or receding from us.

We can also differentiate between different animal calls and the calls of our own species thanks to pitch.

Because we have two ears we can calibrate where a sound is coming from because of the timing in which waves hit each of our eardrums.

It is an effective survival and behavioral tool, but it is a manifestation.

All the information we receive and integrate into our thoughts is colored by the way our brain-sensory organ connection has developed to help us survive and thrive.

Fundamentally we are limited in our ability to process information of our Practical Reality because our brain-sensory organ connection has manifested our own reality from Practical Reality as a survival mechanism, and as elegant as that mechanism is, it limits us in many ways with our connection to the All by creating a new reality within the All that is different from the pure reality of the All.

Touch

As we have previously discussed as it relates to a chair, the particles and charges and space that make up a chair are held together by forces, namely the strong and weak forces, just like we are.

When many atoms approach many atoms, these forces and charges repel each other. We manifest that as "solidness" through our mind nerve connection.

There is no "solidness" at all in True Reality. It exists only in our Practical and Altered Reality.

Yet for many if not most of us, we do not believe something is real unless we can touch it. What we do not think about is that the sensation of touch is a manifestation of our minds like any other manifestation.

Summary

Our senses were created for our survival and not to provide a way for us to connect with the greater quanta of the All or take control of our True Reality.

Our senses provide the information we use to manifest our Practical Reality, but those manifestations evolved for self-preservation not for better understanding our surroundings.

The fact that most of our thoughts come from manifestations of the experience of our senses limits us in terms of being able to relate to our True Reality or to take control of our reality.

These manifestations and thoughts form a core part of our Altered Reality, but are generally not true, meaning they don't exist without our mentalism and are unrelated to the nature of the All without us.

We are left in a complex competition within our own minds, because the same organ that allows us to experience thoughts from our consciousness and connection to the All is overwhelmed by thoughts received by our senses.

Genesis 2:17

"but of the tree of the knowledge of good and evil you shall not eat, for in the day that you eat of it you shall surely die."

Read In Context[1]

---

1. https://www.esv.org/Genesis%202:17/

Chapter 4

The Modifications to Our Practical Reality Caused by the
Development of Our Thought Process

The scientific consensus is that anatomically modern homo sapiens evolved around 300,000 years ago, and behaviorally modern homo sapiens evolved around 50,000 years ago.

As referenced several times before, being alive generally means wanting to stay alive, so for 300,000 years our brains developed processes that are advantageous to our survival.

From a state of consciousness that connected us more closely with our souls, we came to rely on thoughts to protect us as opposed to fangs or claws or venom.

Because we use the same biological device, our brain, that delivers us our consciousness to provide us with protection, our thoughts that we received from our senses compete with the thoughts created by our consciousness making it harder for us to listen to our souls.

In this book I refer to consciousness as our connection to our soul and thereby to the All. We experience thoughts generated by that connection in many forms.

But our survival thoughts are so dominant as biological humans that they often crowd out the important thoughts generated by our consciousness.

Our consciousness at its most limited level is represented graphically in this book as the part of Altered Reality that resides within the pure circle of the All. But our consciousness is not limited by that and, with practice, can extend to the entirety of the All through our souls.

Our biology is our biggest constraint in achieving that connection to our soul because our biology is specific to this Earth Life System and our survival here.

Our manifestations and thoughts derived from our senses crowd out our ability to touch our souls.

Acknowledging that is another critical step in freeing ourselves from those constraints and understanding that most of what we experience and believe is reality is manifested by us, is empowering if we recognize that the manifestation can be in our control.

Our thoughts, and the biological processes our thoughts trigger evolved in an environment that for most of those 300,000 years involved a regular threat of starvation and a corresponding need to conserve energy, regular threats to our existence and a need to survive those threats.

In this Earth life system, we biologically developed a neurotransmitter system that rewarded us for valuable behaviors, fight or flight mechanisms that helped us evade mortal attack, pain triggers and an autoimmune system that helped protect us from injury, hormones that tell us when to eat and when to procreate, emotional and thought processes that conserve energy while building life preserving learning.

We are comprised of millions and millions of systems and processes within us.

None of these systems and processes have to do with our soul, but instead our practical survival here. We have developed these complex systems specifically for self-preservation in this Earth life system. They dominate our lives here and create barriers to our connection to our souls.

Our Practical Reality leaves us believing that only things that we can sense are real. But our Practical Reality is just mentalism and no different than any part of the All including what we cannot sense.

It is our curse to be driven by survival in this Earth life system that we find our Practical Reality more real than the reality it is a subset of.

In this Earth life system, our primal thought processes are those of danger because those thoughts are core to our primal survival directive.

The thought of danger and the corresponding emotion of fear are our strongest thoughts and emotions and the biggest impediments to our connecting with the intuition of our soul and the mentalism of the All.

Scientists call this our negative bias. We are wired to assign greater weight to negative events because they historically were related to our survival, unlike pleasurable events which we assign less value to because we generally survive pleasure.

The thought of danger initiates a chemical and biological fight or flight response through our sympathetic nervous system that we feel as the emotion of fear, and it is critical to survival that that process be quick and energy efficient.

When in mortal danger we need to make quick decisions and conserve our energy for our reaction to the danger threat.

To ensure process speed and energy efficiency, humans evolved into a thought system that repetitively seeks out affirmations regarding the legitimacy of the danger thought/fear emotion and uses that affirmation repetition as its way of providing veracity without requiring thought.

Affirmation works like this. We form a belief about something, let's say that an apple is sweet. Each time that we bite into an apple and find that it is sweet, our thought is affirmed.

The more times we bite an apple and taste that it is sweet, the less we think about whether the apple is sweet and the faster we identify an apple as sweet without even thinking about it.

Emotional affirmations are even more powerful. If we fear ice because we fell once, every time we witness someone falling or fall ourselves after that first time, the quicker we feel fear when we see ice without any thought.

In this way our mind can process stimuli faster using less energy to do so.

In short, instead of thinking, our minds have evolved in a way that lets us create danger thoughts without thinking. This is both a miraculous achievement and a curse that results from our use of our minds as our survival weapon.

In his book "*Thinking, Fast and Slow*" Daniel Kahneman describes the development over time of System 1 and System 2 brain function.

System 1 operates automatically and quickly. System 1 uses little or no energy and has little or no sense of voluntary control. System 1 conserves energy while delivering quick results.

We see an apple and we already know it is sweet because of all the times we have tasted a sweet apple. We similarly know a saber tooth tiger is dangerous because of the times we have been told it is dangerous and the times we have seen it be dangerous.

This is System 1 at work.

System 2 on the other hand uses significant energy allocating attention to the mental activities that demand it. System 2 function is used in things like complex computations and uses energy to ensure thoughtful results.

We try and explain what make an apple taste sweet.

This is System 2 at work.

To be clear, System 1 and System 2 thought are not neurophysiological or morphological processes, but a conceptual terminology developed by Kahneman.

System 1 function is elegant in that it is dependent on thoughts that are tied to emotions and so it looks for emotional affirmation as a way of strengthening its functionality.

As previously discussed, the most significant of those thoughts tied to emotion are danger and fear. We can see this in our everyday lives as a commercial fact – headlines that invoke or affirm fear sell more newspapers than headlines that invoke happiness and peace.

For most of human existence, affirmations were generally slow-paced – there were only so many times we witnessed a saber tooth tiger killing our friend – and over time System 1 built highly valid survival thought responses to stimuli.

These affirmations did not require a separate validation, the repetition of affirmations did that. If we hear or see something enough times, we will believe it is true regardless of whether it is or is not.

It is not happenstance that we feel good when our emotions are affirmed. System 1 evolved to seek out affirmation to reduce the need for verification to make it faster and more energy efficient.

We even developed a pleasure system that rewards us for finding emotional affirmations for System 1. How good does it feel when you see information that validates that something you thought was true is right? "I knew I was right!"

The fight or flight reaction triggered by the thought of danger includes the stimulation of the vagus nerve, the release of hormones like adrenaline and cortisol, and a cascading series of bodily functions all designed to give you the ability to fight or flee: increased blood flow to your muscles, the creation of extra blood sugar to give you instant fuel, activation of your immune system to set up your defenses.

When danger is infrequent, this process triggered by the thought of danger is also infrequent and our bodies are built to have occasional emergencies.

When thoughts of danger are frequent, our bodies tend to get damaged, as we will discuss later, sometimes in irreversible ways.

Kahneman demonstrates that System 1 thinking was necessarily the dominant thought process in humans for most of our existence, and even in a world where System 2 thinking has the luxury of being our primary thought process, we have not evolved as fast as our environment has in that regard.

Testing students believing they were taking tests in university situations, Kahneman and his colleagues found that even when we know that we are being tested on our ability to think with System 2, we more often rely on System 1.

We can't escape the nature of our evolution regarding something that historically was core to our survival in this Earth life system.

Summary

The way we think evolved in a very different world than we exist in today and our thought processes have not evolved as fast as the world around us has.

Our thought systems were built to protect us, not to connect us. The use of our mind as a survival tool in this Earth life system limits our ability to connect to our souls and with the All and crowds out our ability to take control of our reality.

But that is not the end of it. We currently deal with even more limitations caused by our self-made environment in this Earth Life System.

Chapter 5

The Modifications to Practical Reality Caused by Physical Changes in Our Environment

Commercial electricity and various electromagnetic wave forms like radio waves and microwaves developed so quickly around the time of the Industrial Revolution and thereafter, and are so ubiquitous, that we rarely think about them.

But for most of human existence, man-made electromagnetic fields and radio and other waves did not exist.

They are unnatural to this Earth life system.

Our bodies lived in a world with no man-made electromagnetic force or radio or other waves. To say that we are bathed daily in a sea of intense electromagnetic and radio waves would be an understatement.

We believe that our thoughts are biologically controlled by our central nervous system.

By scientific experiment we have proven that our central nervous system is highly sensitive to electromagnetic force and radio frequencies that influence the discharge of the neurons that make up our nervous system.

Scientists believe that neurons discharge chemicals called neurotransmitters that generate electrical signals that then propagate to other neurons creating the biological reality of our thoughts.

Fundamentally, anything environmental that modifies how those electrical signals propagate changes the biology of how we think.

Before industrialization and the advent of massive amounts of environmental electromagnetic force and radio frequencies, human brains necessarily functioned differently biologically.

We likely processed thoughts differently, and while it is scientifically difficult to prove, it seems extremely likely that post industrialization humans and pre-industrialization humans do not think the same way at a biological level.

If time travel were possible and you were to bring a human from the 18th century to this world, the mere electromagnetic and radio wave environment that we live in would be physically assaulting to them.

Before industrialization, we lived in a much different electro-magnetic environment that created resonances that our bodies developed in.

Schumann Resonance

Without manmade background noise, the constant discharge of electricity around the Earth that we witness as lightning creates a resonance called the Schumann Resonance.

The Schumann Resonance is a wave that circles the Earth. Its wavelength is determined by that constant discharge of electricity of lightning strikes.

The Schumann Resonance averages around 7.83hz. That frequency equates to what we manifest as a very, very low musical B note, but it varies around that note depending on global lightning strike frequency, generally running from 7.33hz (a musical B flat) to 8.33hz (a musical C).

The Schumann Resonance is the background noise of this Earth life system without the addition of man-made waves.

The biological firing of neurons in our brains creates electromagnetic wave patterns as well.

The low end of brain Alpha waves falls in the Schumann Resonance range.

Alpha brain waves are a brain wave activity that is associated with restful and meditative states.

Peaceful brain activity is in tune with the background vibrations of the Earth even if inaudible to the human ear. The molecules that make us up still exist and vibrate in it.

For those of us who meditate regularly, it seems natural that we would move into a brain wave pattern that reflects the resonance of the Earth and a modification of that background resonance through manmade electromagnetic and radio wave frequencies may make it harder to find that connection.

In fact, each of the primary brain states has a corollary frequency created by an oscillating voltage produced by the firing of our neurons.

The Gamma band indicates concentration or System 2 brain function.

The Beta band indicates anxiety dominant, active external attention.

The Alpha band indicates relaxed, passive attention.

The Theta band indicates deep relaxation and inward focus.

The Delta band indicates sleep.

These run from highest frequency to lowest frequency.

System 2 thought generates the highest frequency. Thoughts of danger are the second highest.

These brain-emitted frequencies do not exist in a vacuum. They exist in our True Reality because our biological form requires different kinds of brain activities at different times and those activities happen to generate frequencies.

Background vibrations trigger induced and complementary brain wave vibrations, and therefore living in areas with high EMF wave pattens may well trigger brain wave patterns that trigger anxiety.

Manmade EMF

In his book "*The Invisible Rainbow: A History of Electricity and Life*," Arthur Firstenberg explores anecdotal evidence that numerous human maladies have arisen in line with the advent of growth in background electro-magnetic force (EMF).

This background EMF produces arbitrary environmental frequencies that may or may not resonate with the Schumann Resonance and, therefore, are completely unfamiliar to humans at our molecular level and in terms of brain wave patterns.

Firstenberg details an interesting story.

In the early 18th century, a form of capacitor became a party toy for the wealthy. The capacitor was called a Leyden Jar, and it was a way to store static electricity that could be used to provide a small electric shock to those that held onto its anode and cathode.

This is the same kind of shock you can create in the winter by rubbing your flannel pajamas against your sheets and then touching your friend or sibling.

Party guests would gather in a circle holding hands and at the break in the chain one person would touch the cathode of the Leyden Jar and the other the anode and the entire group would receive a static electricity shock.

For some the shock was pleasant fun and for others it made them physically sick.

Firstenberg notes that the electric capacity of these Leyden Jars was far less than that in a modern smart phone.

In just a couple hundred years of a nearly 300,000-year existence, the human body has adapted to a completely foreign environment of electromagnetic noise and energy flowing through our bodies.

At the molecular level we are made up of positively and negatively charged particles and, therefore, we have created an environment that impacts the core of our existence in ways that we cannot possibly measure or comprehend.

At minimum it has changed the biology of how our brains function. it may have altered our molecular biology as well.

Electromagnetic forces and radio waves are not the only changes that the Industrial Revolution brought.

It also brought changes to our environment through the delivery of manmade toxins into the air, soil, and water and into the products we consume.

Ingested Chemicals

During the Industrial Revolution mass production required the introduction of chemicals to protect and enhance the production of crops and livestock, to preserve and alter the appearance of food and drink, to make products that increased revenues.

These chemicals had never been regularly ingested by humans through our breath, skin or digestive systems.

As presented in their paper entitled "Environmental Toxins and Brain: Life on Earth is in Danger," Aggarwal et al. discuss both brain development and brain mutation that is caused by the presence of neurotoxins in the environment.

Many parts of our brains are particularly susceptible to manmade neurotoxins that did not exist for most human existence.

But capitalism and convenience has blinded us to the fact that we would never voluntarily ingest most of these things in any of these ways.

Whether specifically neurotoxin or not, these chemicals have diverse and generally unknown effects in our complex biology leading to any number of health problems from gut biome issues to cancer.

As we have become aware, the neurotransmitters that our body produces that regulate mood and pain, both factors that contribute to our thoughts, are produced though normal bodily functions undisturbed by environmental toxins or inflammatory chemicals.

In his book the *"Mind-Gut Connection,"* Emeran Mayer M.D., eloquently demonstrates how the gut biome and brain constantly communicate causing modifications in how we think and our general health.

Because of the production there of serotonin, the health of our gut biome may have a significant impact on our happiness and emotional well-being.

Even with that knowledge, we consume many chemicals because they exist in the products we buy at supermarkets and believe they must be safe if they are allowed to be sold.

We know that a government body has determined that they do not appear to pose negative health consequence on large population sets, but the anecdotal prevalence of asthma and gut biome issues and other life deteriorating maladies that are not easily diagnosed by modern medicine suggests that chemicals in the air we breathe, chemicals in the foods and drink we consume and chemicals that we inject ourselves with or otherwise absorb have unknown consequences on individuals even if they do not cause significant medical issues for large groups.

In addition to the introduction of chemicals into our food and beverages, certain vulnerabilities in our development were also exploited by companies seeking to get us to consume more of their products.

Our biology developed in ways that rewarded us for finding sweet fruits and vegetables because the sweetness corresponded to vitamins and minerals that helped ensure our vitality.

Coca-Cola once contained cocaine which binds to dopamine and allows it to accumulate in our systems.

In her book *"I'm So Effing Tired: A Proven Plan to Beat Burnout, Boost Your Energy, and Reclaim Your Life,"* Dr. Amy Shah discusses how our pleasure systems were designed over time to reward us for finding and ingesting sweet fruits and vegetables.

The use of sweeteners in food, particularly corn syrup and sugar, allow the manufacturers of food to trigger those biological pleasure responses without any of the nutritional benefits.

We know that high levels of blood sugar damage blood vessels in our brains over time causing brain cells to die that can lead to problems with memory and thought and maybe even lead to dementia.

The use of "empty" calories to increase demand for and ingestion of products leads to numerous other health issues in humans including obesity and diabetes.

The physical changes that we have made in our environment create dramatic modifications to our practical reality leading us into a more and more distant altered reality at a biological level.

Summary

We have created an environment that changes the biology of our thoughts both directly in altering how our neurons fire, and indirectly through biological changes in our bodies that change our internal messaging to our brain.

Our thoughts and thought systems become less capable of connecting with our souls because these environmental factors push us further outside the pure circle of the All into our Altered Reality. But it is not just the environment that we have changed.

We have also changed our information sources moving from nature as our primary source of information to man-made sources of information that further alter our thoughts.

Chapter 6

The Modifications Caused by Manmade Informational Stimulus

Relying entirely on repetitive emotional affirmation as a validation mechanism, as our primary System 1 thought process does, is a massive weakness for humans in this Earth life system in a post-Industrial Revolution world.

The value of System 1 to us is in fact much less than it ever was before, but after hundreds of thousands of years of reliance on it, it is still our dominant thought system.

If you are like me, the information we receive from screens overwhelms the information we receive from the natural world. That is unnatural and not what our sympathetic nervous system is designed to handle

Since System 1 thinking still dominates, those that control manmade sources of information can manipulate our thoughts, sometimes with a different goal in mind, by merely delivering us emotionally affirming information, usually related to our fears because that is our strongest emotion.

When our ancestors witnessed a saber tooth tiger killing a friend, the saber tooth tiger was not lying about that information.

When someone is selling advertisers on their ability to have us watch their content on a screen, the truth of the information being delivered isn't important unless it leads to us choosing to no longer receive that information.

There is a reason why most news headlines are fear invoking.

It feels good at some level for us to find affirmation that our fears are justified because that is how System 1 thinking works to validate danger thoughts.

As we have discussed, our first ancestors developed about 300,000 years ago.

Starting roughly 800 years ago (the invention of the printing press) we began to be conditioned to receive information from what other people wrote.

In roughly the last 100 years we became conditioned to receive near constant information through radios.

In roughly the last 75 years we became conditioned to receive even more information through television.

And in the last 20 years we became conditioned to receive near constant third party and peer-to-peer interactions through smart phones and the Internet.

Screen time is a modern business metric and is tied directly to the revenue of very significant industries. It is important for those businesses to increase screen time and, to do that, they build algorithms that exploit our thought processes.

If you are like most people, the information you receive from screens overwhelms the information you receive from the natural world.

That is unnatural.

The algorithms use the mechanism of our System 1 thought process against us. The algorithms track us, type-cast us and categorize us and then deliver emotional affirmation stimulus to us, often with great rapidity, and with increasing emotional impact without any consideration for veracity of the information.

IBM Watson can determine with high accuracy your personality type with just 3500 of your written words and if you have inadvertently allowed someone who you don't know to follow you on social media, there is a chance that it is just a mechanism to gather your typed words to combine with your Internet search history.

This over-stimulation of System 1 thought processes fills our thoughts with worries and concerns about our Practical Reality.

The algorithms then provide rapid affirmations about those worries and concerns.

Those worries and concerns become more and more important thoughts to us and they form the context and basis for our new thoughts.

Not only is our thought pattern shifted towards more stress and anxiety, but the constant flow of those worries and concerns clouds our ability to disconnect from them.

The combination of pleasure feelings from the affirmations and the increased flow of these thoughts limits our ability to make the correct choices to be our total selves.

Like any addictive substance, social media algorithms make us need more and more emotional affirmation, and as we feed our need for the pleasure we get from emotional affirmation we create more and more distance from our ability to connect with our souls and the reality of the All.

Summary

Beyond the limitations on our reality caused by our location in the All and our biological existence, we are further limited regarding our thoughts.

Our thoughts are manipulated with truths and untruths delivered to us by the screens we watch during the day. These truths and untruths create ideas that build our Altered Reality outside the pure circle of the All. That portion of mentalism is more and more disconnected from the nature of the All.

Since our thoughts make up a large portion of our reality, we are now subject to manipulated thoughts that emphasize our fears and have little if anything to do with the greater reality of the All.

We spend more and more of our time wrapped up in our fears and less and less time connecting to the mentalism of the All and to our souls. We lose faith in our ability to control our reality.

While this manipulation at an individual level is significant, the manipulation across groups is even more significant because its potential to drive us further and further from reality.

Chapter 7

The Modifications Caused by Our Behaviors

Like other animals, we engage in protective behaviors to promote survival. Primal among these is the behavior of tribalism.

Safety in numbers is a behavioral system for all prey animals. It is why we have herds, gaggles, colonies, clutches, and pods.

Unlike other species, self-awareness makes tribalism different for us. We seek the protection of our tribe but, at the same time, we compete within our tribe for status and to avoid rejection. We feel envy. We covet. We fear being alone.

We may also be doing something else. In his book "*Transurfing of Reality*," Vadim Zeland discusses the influence of pendulums, or thought condensate among a group of people.

Thought condensates or "pendulums" develop when tribal members conform to the majority views of a tribe instead of to the intuition of their souls.

Pendulums are a manifestation of System 1 thinking where the System 1 thinking of the members of a tribe have aggregated around the thoughts of a tribal leader or a third party influencing that tribe.

Pendulums draw energy from those who are conforming and take them away from their true and total selves.

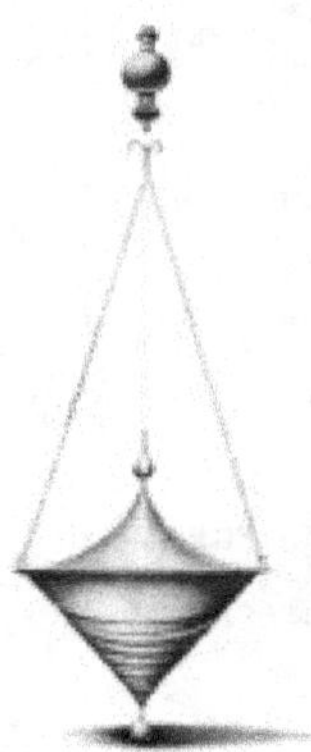

I find the image of a pendulum helpful, as a pendulum consists of a mass at the end of a line with the mass representing the System 1 thought condensate.

The pendulum is made to move by those in control of its motion and all of those who are part of the thought condensate are helpless to its motion.

Like things that we have discussed previously the pendulums pull our Altered Reality even further away from the pure circle of the All because we have let others define our reality for us.

Thought condensates are easy to spot in political parties, but equally present in religions, clubs, fraternities and sororities, families, anywhere that more than one person gathers around a leader or leaders.

Thought condensates even happen in couples.

Most pendulums are destructive because they use people's System 1 fears and insecurities about losing their position in a tribe as a reason for committing their energy to the pendulum.

When we become part of a tribe, we trade conformity for a level of security.

Tribalism is also, therefore, a trade off when it comes to thoughts of danger.

The behavior that reduces external dangers in the same way it does for other animals, replaces those dangers with internal social dangers, and new reasons for fear.

For most of our existence the benefits of tribalism, even with its own perceived dangers, were positive as a species.

They were the result, after all, of hundreds of thousands of years of natural selection.

The balance between social dangers posed by tribalism and the dangers avoided by tribalism on balance were beneficial to humans.

Historically, humans had natural predators that the tribe helped to protect against and status within the tribe was secondary. Today status in the tribe is primary.

Status as a social danger has displaced physical danger creating a fear related to status and that fear creates huge backdoor access to manipulating System 1 thinking.

By way of example, almost everything that happens in modern markets can be explained by two forms of fear: the fear of missing out, commonly referred to as FOMO, and fear, uncertainty, and doubt, commonly referred to as FUD.

These are both modern social fears.

A good real estate broker will always create a perception of limited supply and substantive demand for a property to drive the FOMO of a buyer.

In high school, a popular boy or girl becomes more popular because of FOMO of their peers.

Auctions exist because FOMO is so effective.

Up markets are driven by FOMO and down markets are driven by FUD, but both are core features of the primal human emotion, fear, and are based on the self-awareness that we feel being part of a tribe. Our commitment to the pendulum.

FOMO and FUD are modern versions of the danger thoughts created by behavioral tribalism. "Keeping up with the Joneses," is a statement of tribal danger thoughts.

Suddenly FOMO and FUD become the primal survival instincts necessary to remain a member of, or to retain one's status in, the tribe and they come to dominate our daily thoughts.

Edward Bernays wrote two books in the 1920s, "*Crystalizing Public Opinion*" and "*Propaganda*."

While these books cover many topics, a core theme is the manipulation of the fear of losing standing within the tribe, or worse being rejected by the tribe and left alone.

The book was written long before Kahneman's studies related to System 1 and System 2 functions but demonstrates Bernays' understanding of these issues.

Bernays was a nephew of Sigmund Freud and his writings on influencing public opinion were very influential on Joseph Goebbels who used Bernays ideas to crystalize German public opinion around the Nazi movement.

As a public relations specialist for brands, Bernays ability to tie brands to tribal behavior made him famous. Bernays used his knowledge of tribal behavior and System 1 thinking (though he did not call it that) to build his own "pendulums" for the benefit of his clients.

Goebbels did the same to build thought condensates around the Nazi movement.

During the women's suffrage movement, Bernays hired models to march with protestors smoking Lucky Strike cigarettes.

The models, by definition, represented some aspect of what women aspired to look like and act like and by including them engaging in an activity that involved the product of one of his clients built a pendulum around that activity for that group so that his client could sell more cigarettes.

By combining human tribalism with affirming images that manipulate System 1 thinking, Lucky Strike cigarettes became a symbol of the suffrage movement.

As the middle class began to be defined during the Industrial Revolution, Bernays marketed the existence of a piano in a household as being indicative of being at the higher end of the middle class or upward security in a tribe.

Again, Bernays used a combination of the FOMO of tribalism with the repetitive affirmation of System 1 thinking to create demand for the pianos his client was selling.

As professional associations began to become commercial organizations, Bernays convinced the American Medical Association to define the American breakfast as including a portion of bacon for the benefit of his bacon selling client.

Bernays was a master at creating FOMO in tribes by making members fear that they were not keeping up with the tribe if they did not engage in a certain behavior. He then used System 1 affirmations to direct that behavior.

Bernays knew that by repetitively associating brands, behaviors, and thoughts with tribes, he created a requirement for all tribal members to assimilate. For his corporate customers this meant more sales.

Bernays laid the groundwork for modern social media algorithms.

In investing, tribalism runs rampant. An entire publication called "Value Line" is based on momentum investing, which really means investing in the direction of the investing tribe.

And among funds and fund managers, industries come in and out of favor as do valuation metrics that permeate the "speak" in investor circles. Companies that fit investor FOMO get investments, companies that do not, don't.

We can watch bubbles that follow investor speak: the Internet, Cryptocurrency, Artificial Intelligence where the FOMO spawns both good and bad ideas all chasing the FOMO.

In historic worlds, the combination of the powerful core fear emotion and the propensity towards System 1 dominance worked well because emotional affirmations were generated by the real world and occurred with relative infrequency: seeing a saber tooth tiger initiates a System 1 fear response without any thought and witnessing the tiger attack another animal or a human affirms that emotion.

But in modern worlds, that combination, as evidenced by Edward Bernays in products and brands and by Joseph Goebbels in political power, is highly manipulatable as media increases the pace of emotional affirmation.

There are many modern tools to use to build powerful pendulums quickly.

In very modern worlds, social media as prolifically described in the movie *"The Social Dilemma,"* uses algorithms and information (whether true or false) to affirm emotion to drive advertising revenue.

This kind of rapid-fire System 1 emotional affirmation is overwhelming to a thought process intended to help us quickly trigger our biological fear responses without System 2 thought delays.

In his book *"The Revolt of the Public,"* Martin Gurri discusses the shifting of power to the individual from the politically powerful based on the availability of information.

But there is a deeper point, which is that social media provides a platform for anyone to find a means of emotional affirmation that can manipulate the masses especially if it affirms a powerful emotion that is already prevalent in an existing tribe.

Those tribal members are still biologically built to be rewarded for finding affirmation of their core emotions, but in our modern world those emotions are no longer things like saber tooth tigers, but anything at all because the daily threat of being killed by a saber tooth tiger is gone.

Nevertheless, the same thought triggers are still there. The same pleasure is derived from emotional affirmations for other strong emotions that arise in a modern world.

Dangerously, when you combine anger and fear, you get hate. It is just the other polarity of happiness and peace which gives you love. It is the strong power of the negative pendulum that leads to war.

In this instance the pendulum has pulled Altered Reality so far away from the pure circle of the All that we lose touch entirely with our souls and the All.

In the Clinton-Trump election, the Trump tribe's primary emotion was hate for Clinton and the Clinton tribe's primary emotion was hate for Trump. That negative pendulum was easy to build quickly on either side.

The social media algorithms understand that to maintain someone's attention, the emotional affirmation needs to get stronger and stronger, and so we wind up with absurd affirmations that exacerbate hate.

A Trump tribesperson absolutely believes that Clinton is running a prostitute ring out of a pizza parlor because of the biological satisfaction it creates, and a Clinton tribesperson absolutely believes that Trump is incontinent and wears diapers while playing golf.

Through experiments, Kahneman found that truth was irrelevant in emotional affirmation. We prefer emotional validation to the truth because historically our survival needed to reward us for emotional affirmations and not for System 2 fact validation.

As information sources using artificial intelligence get better and better at using System 1 processes against humans, the most powerful pendulums they can build are negative energy pendulums in tribes and those create altered realities that are so narrow as to prohibit an ability to find our way to the reality of the All and the power and happiness of being our total selves.

We live in more and more fear and more and more stress.

Summary

The combination of our continued dependence on System 1 thinking and the modern reality of tribalism have driven us so far away from reality that without understanding all the issues with our altered reality, it is nearly impossible to find our way back to reality and living in the limitless energy fields and other planes of existence offered by the All.

We are further distanced from our soul and the intuition that our soul provides.

We are further distanced from taking control of our reality.

Chapter 8

Stress, Anxiety and Fear

When we are living only in our Altered Reality, life is out of balance. As our Altered Reality limits us more and more from connection to our soul, life becomes more out of balance because our life choices are more disconnected from the intuition provided by our soul making our actions seem more happenstance.

This lack of balance leads to mental, emotional, and physical issues for our biological existence in this Earth life system.

Andrew Bernstein's book *"The Myth of Stress"* eloquently discusses one of the core problems with modern environment and the evolution of thought. As Bernstein points out, the word "stress" is a modern concept, one that arose after the Industrial Revolution.

In this Earth life system, we have used "stress" to describe physical pressure, like the pressure of the roof on the frame of a house. But in industrialized times, we needed a word to describe a new reality – the overstimulation of the fear trigger through non-life-threatening events.

When humans are not faced with saber tooth tiger threats on a regular basis and when tribal social stresses and contributing emotional energy to social pendulums, the thought process related to fear trigger can identify many stimuli as being fear triggers: traffic jams, disputes at work, social media slights.

Modern psychologists and mindset coaches call these things trauma, which is just a term used to describe stimuli that in a modern world result in fight or flight triggers.

Our bodies are not built to be in a constant state of fight or flight, but when the thought process that initiates the fear emotion is constantly being stimulated to believe a fight or flight response is required, the body responds with more constant activation of fight or flight mechanisms than were ever intended.

As Bernstein points out, taking control of that initial thought process to unlearn thoughts that trigger fear can stop that stress in its tracks, but over a lifetime there can be so many triggers that unlearning can be hard work and permanent or very difficult to alter biological changes may have already occurred.

Moreover, as I have discussed in this book, our Altered Reality takes the fears we have and amplifies them. The effect is like a strong wind on a forest fire. Containing that fire can become a lifelong pursuit.

As discussed earlier in this book, there is a cascade effect of biological, chemical, and neurological things that happen in our bodies in response to the thought of fear.

Heightened cortisol levels have been associated with inflammation of the digestive tract which can dramatically affect the proper functioning of your gut biome.

Gut biome issues can lead to digestive issues discomfort that can cause other stress responses.

Gut biome issues can also alter serotonin production leading to a host of other complications including pain loops.

Other fight flight mechanisms can over stimulate your auto-immune system leading to complications and can affect the muscles of your intestines.

Visceral hypersensitivity triggers pain responses that can lead to chronic pain issues.

Vagus nerve stimulation can become chronic, making us feel constantly on edge and much more reactive to new stimuli.

All of these things can lead to responsive emotional and psychological problems that can create a circularity.

Many people suffer from forms of gut biome dysfunction. Beyond the digestive issues, pain, bloating, the gut is also critical to proper neurotransmitter function.

The combination leads to general misery that further modifies reality.

The modern version of this Earth life system is a complex place for extremely well-developed biological humans who pulled their own environmental rug out from under their feet.

Health issues, fears and overwhelming amounts of sensory stimulation further focus us on some limited and possibly warped version of our practical reality and pull us further and further away from our greater reality.

Chapter 9

Faith

Where does our certainty end and our faith begin? In many ways the answer to that question defines the boundaries of our manifested reality.

We have already determined that everything in our Altered Reality is a manifestation of our minds.

If you think about those manifestations, they are supernatural and magical. We take a boson called a photon and we manifest it into light and color, beauty and emotion.

We do the same with the collision of obvious matter hitting our ear drums. We manifest those into sound and music, beauty, dissonance, and emotion.

It doesn't take any faith for us to be magical in those ways.

But we don't intentionally manifest when we manifest light, color and sound.

That doesn't mean that we can't. But why does it seem like we must have faith to do that?

When we struggle with faith, what are we really struggling with? We already perform the miraculous every day.

But in our Altered Reality we limit ourselves and everything outside those limitations requires faith.

The word faith, therefore, defines the starting point of our self-made limitations and fears.

As we have discussed, our reality is a manifestation of our mind - sensory organ connection altered by many things that impact how we biologically and practically think.

Our Altered Reality pushes us into our practical survival, into biological changes, into manipulations of our thought systems, into pendulums.

We feel out of control and look to things like science to make us feel in control.

Because math can express everything from negative infinity to positive infinity, we can create mathematical models to explain anything, but we can't use mathematical models to define anything, merely predict that an existence is possible or probable.

Everything in our lives requires some degree of what we think of as faith because everything in our lives is a manifestation of our minds.

Passive manifestation we believe to be reality. Intentional manifestation we believe requires faith.

They are the same except that they differ in direction.

Passive manifestation is manifestation of things received by us: it faces outward.

Intentional manifestation is manifestation of things beyond our consciousness: it faces inward.

Because intentional manifestation is inward through our consciousness to our soul and the All, it is dependent on the nature of the All.

For example, when a surfer goes to manifest a great surf session, the surfer is entirely dependent on the waves that are available.

No two waves are exactly alike and a surfer's ability to exactly replicate a ride on two different waves is impossible.

At every moment in our timeline there is a different existence of energies and planes of existence as they are not static, requiring a different choice to manifest.

You cannot ask a surfer to replicate a ride on a flat day or even on the very next wave any more than you can ask anyone to replicate an interaction with the energies of the universe once that moment has passed.

Accordingly, there are no affirmations for our ability to intentionally manifest because no two instances in time will be the same.

The great challenge for us in accepting what I am telling you is that what we view as certainty is merely those things that we have the most affirmations for from our lives in Altered Reality.

As we have discussed, our primary System 1 thinking is biologically built to look for affirmation.

Mystical things like contact with the dead, connection to our soul, intuition, manifestation have few if any daily affirmations.

But it does not mean that we are not all capable of them. As we have already determined, we are capable of magical things when we manifest.

An ability to move through time and space, or exist in two or more places in time and space, visit a different plane of existence are things that science predicts as possible in quantum physics, but we don't receive affirmations about our ability to do that with our System 1 thoughts.

Unfortunately, our daily affirmations come from our Altered Reality and so they make us believe that they are truer than any other reality.

We see the bright light of the sun on a cloudless morning, the blue of the morning sky, the music of birds chirping, the smell of coffee and bacon.

They reaffirm in us that all those things are real.

But, as we have discussed, those are all manifestations.

The only true reality is that of the All, and it is infinite, but because of how we are biologically created, our soul and the All feel like the things we need to have the most faith to believe in.

They are where our belief must start.

Chapter 10

Mentalism and Hermetic Principles

We discussed mentalism earlier in this book.

Mentalism means that everything is a creation of the mind of the All including the All, just like light and color are a creation of our mind.

This is not to say that the All has a brain, but that the nature of the reality of the All is the same as the nature of the reality of our consciousness and our thoughts.

This book provides a good illustrative example of mentalism.

Every word, sentence, concept that I have written in this book existed in my mind without my writing them down.

The book is a convenience that permits a broad audience to use their senses - photons hitting their retina if a physical or digital book, soundwaves hitting their ear drums if an audio book - to bring my reality into their minds.

If we could easily read minds, the physical book wouldn't be necessary.

Its existence already existed in the mentalism of the All through my mentalism before it was written. The limitations on our ability to read minds is created by our own self-limiting beliefs and thoughts that do not exist in the All.

My existence is defined by me by the same consciousness and thoughts that created this book. My reality is based on mentalism just like the All.

This may feel hard to grasp, but everything we experience in this Earth life system is only real to us because of our consciousness and our thoughts. We live our lives exactly like the reality of the All.

But as I have demonstrated through earlier chapters in this book, because our biological evolution resulted in our use of thoughts for survival, because of the limitations of our true, practical, and altered reality, we limit ourselves through disbelief regarding what is real.

In the mid 1990s, Nobel Laureate mathematical physicist, Sir Roger Penrose, and Dr. Stuart Hameroff proposed an alternate theory of consciousness.

Modern science had up to that point described consciousness across many competing theories, most of which looked at the combination of millions of neurons firing in the brain.

The theory proposed by Penrose and Hameroff is called Orchestrated Objective Reduction Theory (Orch OR) and it theorizes that consciousness is created at a quantum level suggesting that consciousness is integrated into a quantum "consciousness" throughout the universe through quantum physics.

Essentially Penrose and Hameroff are saying exactly what Hermetics have taught, which is that our consciousness is part of the mentalism of the All. They just use theories of physics to say that.

For Penrose and Hoffman consciousness is something that exists as a quantum physics reality, and it explains scientifically connections to the universe that we perceive.

Earlier I discussed how photons were the logical choice for sight because of the speed at which they travel and the wavelength information that they deliver.

But have you ever "sensed" something coming before you saw it, heard it, felt it, smelled it or tasted it?

Quantum mechanics has several interesting properties including the ability to alter the rate of the passage of time through speed and mass, the ability for an existence in more than one place at once which is called quantum superposition and other concepts that we would otherwise view as occult or supernatural.

If consciousness is quantum, there are scientifically no limitations to the expansion of consciousness.

Remote viewing, manifestation, creation, intuition, communication with those on other planes of existence are all possible.

Mentalism is the primary nature of the reality of the All.

Within that primary nature there are certain rules that govern how mentalism operates and those rules manifest themselves in the nature of everything that exists within the All.

The Principle of Correspondence

The concept of "as above, so below."

There is a correspondence between every plane of existence, every energy and energy field. They all exist together in the mentalism of the All.

In our practical world, we have explored how unhealthy thoughts limit healthy biology in our bodies and vice versa. But this is merely an example of a much deeper and broader concept.

Our soul exists on every plane of existence and in every energy and energy field of the All.

To live an intentional total life, our conscious existence in all of those places must be aligned.

As above, so below. As below, so above.

When we are not aligned, we work on one plane without listening to other planes, we fail to heed our intuition or our soul, we find life to be full of chance because we are not living in correspondence.

We can see correspondence in successful people. We are often drawn to them because we can feel the correspondence of their lives.

For most of us, we fail to understand or work for that correspondence because of self-limiting thoughts, thoughts that we deserve to be punished, fear, self-doubt, questions of self-worth.

For some, finding our way to correspondence comes more naturally and for others it is harder, but it is the same for all of us and it is a core rule of reality.

Accordingly, hard work is not enough in life. Effective work requires correspondence.

The Principle of Vibration

Everything vibrates. At very small scales we are made up of particles that are constantly moving and interacting with forces and force-communicating particles.

Everything that makes up the All is in constant motion, some at nearly zero pace and others at near infinite pace and everything in between.

Different planes of our existence are characterized by different vibrations. We sense those vibrations sometimes when we feel connections to other energies.

Because everything is in motion, the scientific concept of validation of interaction with the other planes of existence and energies of the All is invalid, because every interaction is infinitely different. There is no controlled experimentation.

Often we believe that because something cannot be scientifically proven it cannot be real, but what I have just shown you is that reality has no static environment in which science can generate any valid result regarding the nature of the All.

The Principle of Polarity

Everything is dual. Everything has a duality made up of polar, opposites and everything in between.

Opposites are the same and only vary in degree. For example, black and white are the same with black representing an absence of white, white representing an absence of black and everything in between being a degree of each.

We think of polarities in our Altered Reality as for example love and hate on the emotional, mental level, good and evil on a moral level. But these are manifestations of our Altered Reality mentalism.

The polarities of the All are things like peaks and troughs, positive and negative, male and female. It is important to understand that distinction as our Altered Reality mentalism traps us into belief systems that lie outside the pure circle of the All.

You cannot get rid of polarities, but you must understand them as it relates to intuition.

The Principle of Rhythm

Everything has a rhythm: ebb and flow, pendulum right and left.

For everything there is an action and a reaction. Understanding this nature of the universe is critical to understanding the nature of the motion of the universe.

Ebbs and flows manifest in our Altered Reality as good days and bad days, but good and bad are our manifestations.

The ebb and flow of the All is one of energies and is critical to our understanding of intuition.

Manifestation and creation can only happen when the energies of the All are flowing towards that manifestation or creation.

The Principle of Cause and Effect

Every cause has its effect. Nothing is random. Anything that appears as chance has a cause at some plane of existence, or some combination of planes of existence.

Understanding this principle means that we can see that our altered reality makes it very hard for us to understand our lives because we have no connection to causal planes outside our altered reality.

We can only experience them through the intuition provided by our soul.

The Principle of Gender

There is a duality in every act of creation. The element of intention and the element of production.

We often refer to these as "male" and "female" elements and without a correspondence between the two we cannot manifest our intentions.

Nothing can be created on any plane without understanding that creation requires a masculine and a feminine element.

The feminine element is the element from which things are created and flow like the cathode of a battery, and the masculine element is the element that draws out the creation and flow.

When I write this book, my writing comes from my feminine element and thoughts that are drawn out by my masculine element, my consciousness during my meditations.

At our core we are made up of masculine and feminine elements at the atomic level: electrons (feminine) and protons (masculine).

We are all both masculine and feminine inside and have to understand that correspondence to understand how we manifest things in our lives.

Consciousness and thought are a gender combination, and our Altered Reality breaks that combination by limiting our thoughts.

Now that we have explored both the nature of our internal mentalism, where it comes from and how it limits us, as well as the nature of the All, we are ready to do the work of finding our way back to manifesting our own realities and connecting to our soul and the All.

When we manifest our own reality and connect with our soul, we create joy, success, happiness and peace because we are taking control of our existence on every level and creating the reality we want to and are meant to exist in

PART 2

A surfer stands on the shore in New Jersey as a hurricane runs hundreds of miles off the coast.

The waves are strong and large, and to surf the waves, the surfer needs to paddle out about 200 yards through the waves to get to the first wave break.

She watches the water. There are an incalculable number of changes going on in the water.

She knows that the water that comes in must also go back out. She looks for a rip current. It can appear in one place and move to another place.

For a swimmer, the rip current is dangerous, for the surfer, it is her pathway through the waves.

When she sees it, if she hesitates, it may move before she can take advantage of it. If she makes a mistake and misreads the rip current, she will be punished by the incoming waves.

Only her intuition can guide her, but her mind will question whether she is making the right choice because it fears the punishment of the waves.

Her intuition processes the cumulation of everything that is happening in the water: the changing tide, the changing wind, the vibration of the water, the ebb and flow of the water coming into shore and heading back out to sea, the nature of the waves, the interaction of the water with the ocean floor, and the causes and effects and correspondences of all of these things to name a few.

Will she listen to her intuition, or will she let her doubts, fear and limiting thoughts win even though she knows that only her intuition can guide her?

The surfer and we face the same dilemma every moment of our lives. Do we listen to our intuition, or do we listen to our doubts, fear and limiting thoughts?

Fear and survival thoughts of our Practical Reality are so powerful they keep us from listening to what we know through our souls, just like the surfer who knows through her experience may hesitate because of fear.

We finished Part 1 with an exploration of the Hermetic principles for a reason. The Hermetic principles show how complex the nature of the All is at any point in time – so complex that we cannot use our System 2 thought to calculate them fast enough.

Only through our soul and the intuition it provides can we understand the governing principles of the All at every decision point, and at every decision point our barriers, limiting thoughts and fears that are the hallmark of our Altered Reality will fight our ability to do so.

We are the only thing that stands in our own way of manifesting our own realities in ways that we want.

In Part 1, we worked down from the All to our Altered Reality to understand that our Altered Reality that we spend most of our time in is a very limited part of the mentalism of the All.

Worse, our Altered Reality pulls us away from the reality of the All and makes it harder for us to connect to our soul and the critical intuition it provides by creating blockades through fears and limiting doubts.

Much of our Altered Reality is baggage that we need to shed because it makes us believe that we are not in control of our own reality.

I cannot say this enough.

We are magical.

We create our physical existence though what we eat, drink and breathe. From those things we create a heart, a brain and everything else in us.

We manifest miracles every day through our mind-sensory organ connection. We create things that do not exist without us. We create light, color, beauty, music and love. We create the opposites as well.

The term supernatural is an odd term. Nearly our entire Altered Reality is supernatural, meaning it is a manifestation unexplainable by the laws of nature.

We create what does not exist without us and other sentient beings every moment of every day but trap ourselves into believing that only certain miraculous manifestations are possible, and others are not.

Anything is possible within the rules of the All, and we are all capable of living our lives in a reality that we intentionally manifest if we do not let the limitations, doubts and fears of our Altered Reality hold us back.

As Zeland suggests in his book, it is a surprisingly simple concept to live our total life in that all it requires is manifesting, creating, and making choices by listening to our soul.

But what Zeland does not say is how hard it is to get to the point of listening to our soul and truly believing what it is telling us because the baggage of our Altered Reality is constantly fights us.

The ability to listen to our souls and the intuition they provide us and recognize that we have created our Altered Reality ourselves is the critical basis for living a total life.

As we discussed at the beginning of this book, our souls are connected to the All and know the All intimately. Our soul is what provides us with the guidance in making choices consistent with the nature of the All.

At any point in time our soul makes it easy to understand the nature of the All, where understanding the All through methods in our Altered Reality is practically impossible.

Intentionally living through manifestation and creation involves both proactive receiving and proactive work.

Intention requires energy and we are preprogrammed, as we have discussed, to conserve energy. We must recognize that intention is one of the most valuable uses of our energy.

We are all capable of training our minds through practice to move away from barriers, fears and limiting thoughts created by our Altered Reality and back into consciousness that connects us to other planes of existence, other energies, and energy fields.

By building those connections we can gain balance, control, happiness and even bliss in our lives.

We can dream to be many things, but if those dreams derive from our Altered Reality, what yogis might refer to as our karma, we either will not succeed or not be happy.

In our Altered Reality we carry baggage that makes us desire things for reasons that have nothing to do with our true selves and our souls, like the expectations of others, or false perceptions of ourselves that evolved through life experiences to name two.

The initial journey is to clear away this baggage so that we can find the pathway back to our intuition, because without our intuition we cannot make choices that are resonant with both our true selves and the nature of the All.

We can manifest and create nearly anything in our life so long as it is consistent with our true selves and the nature of the All.

Without being able to listen to the intuition of our soul, we are merely guessing at our life choices.

Instead, if we focus on the pattern of our soulful intuition and from that intentionally manifest our present, we will find ourselves in a constant state of gratitude for the opportunity that living intentionally provides.

Just like the surfer in the example at the beginning of this Part 2, along the way, the limitations of our Altered Reality thoughts may cause us to question our journey. Do not let them.

The All is not bound by time. The intuition provided by our souls may involve a destination of mind, spirit, body or work, but there is no reason to believe that the journey to that destination will be linear in terms of the time here in this Earth life system.

For instance, our intuition may tell us that a particular investment is very good. That investment may go down before it goes up.

A business we believe we must create could be lost before the right business emerges from it. The only thing that makes the path mysterious is the limitations of our Altered Reality.

Never be dissuaded when you know you are listening to the intuition of your soul.

Chapter 11

Regulating Our Inputs

To clear out the thought and biological limitations that hinder our ability to connect with the intuition provided by our soul, we must go back through those things that cause those limitations.

Our Altered Reality creates many emotional belief systems that combat our ability to live our total lives.

We must work to get rid of much of that part of our Altered Reality that lies outside the pure circle of the All.

These limited emotional states are frequently tied to a silent belief that we don't deserve something or should be punished in some way which overrides our ability to make choices based on our intuition: guilt, superiority, inferiority, discontent, idealization, contempt, excessive desire, and perfectionism all result in some form of punishment thought.

Punishment thoughts are insidious. Sometimes we know we are having them, other times they are subconscious.

Either way, punishment thoughts are those thoughts that tell us that we don't deserve something or, worse, that we deserve punishment.

They make us not believe in the intuition of our soul or disregard it because we do not believe that we deserve what we can achieve if we listen.

But even before we get to dealing with those thoughts, we must start by freeing our biological brain from environmental factors that impact its biological function.

Taking Control of What We Ingest

While there is little that we can do to practically manage some of the biological and chemical inputs that we exist in, things like electromagnetic force, radio waves and the existence of environmental toxins and neurotoxins that are in our environment regardless of our choice, the most significant biological and chemical input we receive is through what we ingest.

In yoga, our physical bodies are referred to as our food bodies because our entire physical nature is derived from what we eat, breathe and drink.

What we ingest is almost completely in our control and has significant impact on our healthy biological and neurological function that is at the core of our biological existence.

Our consciousness manifests in thoughts just like our sense manifest in thoughts. When our brain function is limited, it impacts our ability to find our way to our true selves through our soul.

Much has been written in the media about high processed foods. Processed foods are foods created by industrialization that has led to our ingesting many things we would never dream of ingesting but that are deemed "safe" to ingest by some government authority.

Our neurotransmission system only functions correctly when our gut biome and the rest of our biome is functioning correctly. Our neurons that generate our thoughts are regulated by our neurotransmission system. A significant part of that system is based on a healthy functioning gut.

Taking back control of our lives and finding our way back to our souls starts with something simple: eating and drinking things that are not poisoning us and biologically altering our thoughts.

This sounds easier to do than we think. Outside of water, there is no beverage that our body needs. Even water can be full of chemicals and other agents that we would never voluntarily choose to ingest.

Culturally we have adopted drinking other beverages – teas, sodas, coffees, wines, other alcohols, juices. Some of these may have health benefits, some others may not, and everything is subject to portion size, but all we need is water.

Think about what you drink before you drink it. Many drinks contain large amounts of forms of sugar that are tied to dopamine stimulation that was originally intended to ensure that we were getting a diversity of vitamins and minerals in our diet.

Excessive amounts of sugar do nothing for us other than damage our brains and cause disease.

Things we ingest can change our emotions and change our biology which modifies our Altered Reality in ways that make it harder for us to connect to our soul because our emotions and biological changes dominate our thoughts.

Food is also regulatable. Here is a simple rule: Don't eat anything that contains any ingredient that you would not voluntarily ingest on its own.

Many foods have been shown to harm brain function and thought including foods made with industrial and processed seed oils, foods with added and refined sugars, processed foods, foods with artificial sweeteners, fried foods.

Don't eat them – or at least avoid them as much as you can.

There are numerous chemicals that are used to stabilize, preserve, enhance the flavor of and trigger dopamine dependency in foods we eat.

Don't eat them - we have no idea what they do to us or our bodies.

Maintain your blood pressure at normal levels because high blood pressure alters brain function and leads to other medical conditions that can alter your emotions and biological function.

Consider eating foods that have been proven to enhance brain health.

Leafy greens such as kale, spinach, collards, and broccoli are rich in brain-healthy nutrients like vitamin K, lutein, folate, and beta carotene.

Fatty fish are abundant sources of omega-3 fatty acids, healthy unsaturated fats that have been linked to lower blood levels of beta-amyloid—the protein that forms damaging clumps in the brains of people with Alzheimer's disease.

Berries are abundant in flavanoids, the natural plant pigments that give berries their brilliant hues, also help improve memory, research shows.

The caffeine in your morning cup of coffee or tea leads to better mental function and possibly helps solidify new memories.

Nuts are excellent sources of protein and healthy fats, and walnuts in particular might also improve memory.

Maintaining the normal function of our biological existence allows us to be conscious and think without biological limitation or, at least, with as little biological limitation as possible.

When our biology is stabilized, it is time to start working on our thoughts to unload the baggage of our Altered Reality.

Taking Control of Thoughts

As Kahneman has described to us, not all our thoughts are the same. The thought function we need to cultivate is our System 2 thought. It is the active thought process.

System 2 uses energy and we have been trained over hundreds of thousands of years to use it sparingly. It is the part of our thought that intentionally delivers instead of automatically delivering. The anode to the System 1 cathode. The Hermetic male to the System 1 female.

For most if not all of us, we allow the System 1 cathode to dominate because we have been trained to do so. Unfortunately, in this modern world, we have taught machines how to regulate and manipulate our System 1 thinking for profit.

We need to recognize all of this and stop it.

Most of us humans do not live in a world anymore where we need to conserve mental energy or where we need a quick reaction to survive.

System 1 thinking is an artifact, still useful, but allowing it to be dominant when we have created machines that manipulate it, is enslaving us, making us feel that we are not in control of our reality, pulling our Altered Reality further away from the pure circle of the All and further away from connection with our souls.

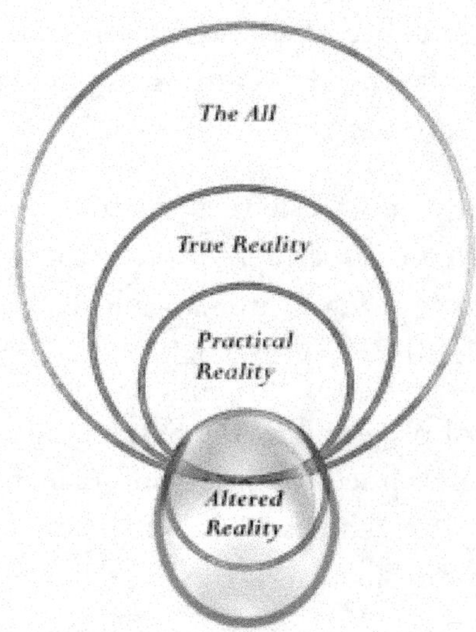

We are left empty and lost.

Most of us have lived some extensive amount of our lives allowing ourselves to be dominated by System 1 thinking and, for the last 25 or so years we have been subject to massive amounts of affirmations that have formed the core of our System 1 emotional reactions.

Most of those affirmations need to be unlearned, and System 2 is what we must rely on to do that.

To take back control of our thoughts and our reality, we must reverse engineer what we have created: a massive amount of baggage in the form of Altered Reality, some portion of which exists merely to create profits for companies and has nothing to do with us intentionally creating our reality.

The process we need to engage in is like many other processes, particularly those involved in performance-based activities.

We need to exert a lot of energy in building skills to get to a point where it comes naturally to us not to live in the Altered Reality we have built for ourselves.

Some can do this without meditation, just a conscious acceptance. Others, like me, require meditation.

In the end we must unwind all those fears and limitations that have been created within us and move back into the pure circle of the All.

Step1 Stopping the Growth of Altered Reality – Shutting Off the Spigot

We start with the spigot that feeds the growth of our Altered Reality and then we move to the bucket that is our Altered Reality.

The spigot is made up of two streams. One is the stream of information that we receive from unnatural, manmade, sources. The other is our situational environment by which I mean our genetics, the people, creatures and environment around us.

First, we work on the manmade sources because while they may be hard to root out, they are more controllable.

To do this, we must do something uncomfortable and exhausting which is to use our System 2 thinking to analyze our System 1 thinking.

As we discussed earlier in the book, System 2 thinking is analytic, proactive and energy consuming while System 1 thinking is reactive, emotional, and low energy consumption.

But even though System 1 thinking is low energy to use, it is high energy to unwind because it was our historic source of protection.

Working from the outside in, we start with the biggest manmade influences on our System 1 thinking that we previously referred to as thought condensates, or Zadim pendulums.

We can find the pendulums that influence our System 1 thinking relatively easily. Our pendulums are System 1 thoughts and emotions that are intense and that are being manipulated by something or someone else.

Our System 1 thinking is the female element in the Hermetic sense and reacts to stimulation by male elements.

In the case of pendulums, the male element is a tribal leader or an algorithm that has identified us as part of a tribe and uses emotional affirmations related to those tribal belief systems to keep us engaged.

Perform a tribal inventory by writing down the tribes we consider ourselves a part of: our political party, our religion, our gender, race and age, any other groups we identify ourselves with.

Next, identify the ways we receive our information: what news channels do we watch, what newspapers do we read, what social media do we follow.

We then do what we normally do, we read, listen, or watch the information delivered to us. But this time, any time that we feel an emotional rise or affirmation from some information that we receive, we write it down.

We keep a log indicating the source of the information received, the message contained and the level of emotional stimulation we received.

This log begins to define for us the pendulums and System 1 affirmations that are shaping our Altered Reality beyond those created by our situational environment.

When performed for a week, review the content that is causing the largest emotional stimulation and reflect over what it is about that content that was so significant, and which tribe that content pertains to.

Do this exercise again the following week and the week after that.

What emerges is a picture of our pendulums, where our System 1 thinking is being dominated by others.

We are recognizing in ourselves what things delivered by social media and other media channels trigger us most. It can be helpful to examine the messaging to see if it is verifiable or merely manufactured to create the reaction in us.

Remember that our System 1 thinking does not have a separate verification system outside of affirmation and it will opt for affirmation over truth because verification requires energy and is a System 2 thinking function.

Our System 1 thinking will fight our System 2 analysis.

Don't let it. System 1 thinking is a useful evolutionary artifact of survival and, while still necessary, it should no longer be dominant.

We are reverse engineering the media algorithms so that we can undo their modifications to our Altered Reality that enter through System 1 thought manipulation, and we are affirmatively engineering our minds towards System 2 dominance.

It is the only way for us to start to take control of our reality because to do that we must shed large portions of our Altered Reality that are managed by our System 1 thinking.

Knowing where we are most open to System 1 affirmation stimulation is critical to unwinding the thoughts related to unnatural stimuli, and to unwinding our fears and limiting thoughts and beliefs.

By writing this process down, we give it a separate existence in our Altered Reality. That separate existence is something that we can learn to shed.

Based on our analysis, we use the knowledge we gain to avoid that messaging from media, or better, analyzing that information with System 2 thinking instead of merely receiving it through System 1 thinking.

For some of us it might mean disconnecting from the media altogether.

If we work at this long enough, we begin noticing that we have strong emotions built up over time that our System 1 thinking will fight to hold on to, because that is what System 1 thinking is designed to do.

These strong emotions are our prisons and keep us from intentionally creating our own reality because they require us to live in their reality.

We must break out of the cycle of negative pendulums and System 1 emotional affirmation if we want to tap the supernatural of our souls and the intuition it provides for our manifestation and creation.

When we have worked through our manmade pendulums, we then focus on the other part of the spigot.

That part of the spigot is personal, and it relates to how we manifest our own existence in our situational environment.

The amazing thing about this part of the spigot is that our individual existence relative to everything and everyone else is entirely in our control even though we generally do not realize that.

We might believe that certain things "trigger" us, but the reality is we manifest everything, and the labeling of a "trigger" is just a way of us protecting our System 1 thinking from our System 2 thinking.

Because we are so reliant on System 1 thinking, we rarely proactively choose how we manifest information in our daily lives.

But we must, to move towards manifesting our reality.

This part of spigot management is individual.

It is a personal journey based on our individual situational environment for each of us to begin to realize how much control we have over our own manifestation.

Everything we experience is just an experience. How we manifest that experience is up to us.

That realization is the only awareness we need to manifest that within us. But we have to believe it.

While this process may take some time, turning off the spigot that is feeding our Altered Reality is critical to our ability to focus on the Altered Reality it has already created.

It is a practice, and it may never be perfect, but by doing it we begin to bring our Altered Reality back towards the pure circle of the All.

We are, therefore, turning off this spigot so that we can deal with the bucket.

Step2 Ridding Oursleves of our Altered Reality – Fixing the Bucket

Years or a lifetime spent in our situational environment with manmade information being constantly delivered to us has filled us with emotional, biological, and thought-based limitations that make us feel like we cannot control our reality.

These limitations are baggage and may not be simple to clear away.

Yoga refers to this baggage as karma and it can be gained in this lifetime, it can be generational, and it can be both.

Anxiety, guilt, superiority, inferiority, discontent, idealization, contempt, excessive desire, and perfectionism can hide way beneath the surface, and they will limit or even halt your ability to listen to your intuition and make choices based on that intuition.

There is no magic pill to work through these issues and every human is different.

Learning how to believe that we do not deserve punishment in any form is a personal journey.

Learning that we are not limited and are in full control of manifesting our reality is also a personal journey.

I have used both therapy and meditation to get to that state, but mindset training may also be valuable as well as other practices like yoga.

Some may be able to do this simply through understanding and System 2 self-analysis.

Whatever works for you. If you haven't rooted these limitations out, you will find them along the way, and you will always have an opportunity to resolve them.

This is work and practice and it does not end because we continue have System 1 thoughts and we continue to live in our situational environment and receive manmade information.

We need to give ourselves the grace to understand that and not be dissuaded from continuing with our work and practice.

The truth is that we are only limited by our own thoughts and fears. Our consciousness, the intuition of our soul and its connection to the All are boundless.

Chapter 13

Mentalism, Intuition and The Basics of Tapping into the Supernatural

The First Three Steps

As we explored through much of Part 1 of this book, everything we experience in our Altered Reality is through thoughts generated by our mind-sensory organ interactions, the interactions of our minds with environmental stimuli and through how our thought processes developed and are manipulated.

In short, we have discussed how our reality is self-made and is very limited compared to the reality of the All and is often extended beyond the pure circle of the All in ways that make it harder for us to connect to our souls.

But our Altered Reality is a mirror, as well as a subset of the All.

Our reality is entirely based on our thoughts.

Color, light, taste, scent, sound, touch are all mental creations. They do not exist in the All without our mentalism.

Similarly, nothing exists without the mentalism of the All.

We derive thoughts from our soul through our consciousness just like we derive thoughts from our senses, it is just that the thoughts from our senses tend to overwhelm, limit, or deny the thoughts we derive from our souls.

Our mentalism, therefore, often limits our ability to accept and exist in the mentalism of the All and to understand and accept that manifesting our reality is in our control.

To live our truest life to the fullest, we need to unload the baggage of our Altered Reality, accept our ability to manifest our reality and find our way to the mentalism of the All because that is where we find our soul and the intuition that guides us to make choices at each stage of our lives that lead to manifestation, creation and the supernatural.

So where do we start engaging our mentalism now that we have addressed the spigot and bucket of our Altered Reality?

To get to someplace that fulfills us, we need to first know where we are starting from and what fulfills us. Meditating on who we are and what brings us bliss is a critical first step to intentional manifestation.

When we know who we are and what brings us bliss, we can begin to listen to the guidance of our intuition.

Meditating on the pattern of our intuitive experiences moves us into a state of correspondence that guides our intentional manifestation.

But first we must prepare our minds and consciousness for that journey.

The most important step first meditative step is clearing our minds of what remains of our Altered Reality because the noise of our Altered Reality gets in the way of truly exploring our conscious connections to the All, our soul and the intuition provided by our soul.

While in a perfect world it would be wonderful to exist in a state where we have unloaded all the baggage of our Altered Reality so that it does not exist at all, the reality for most of us is that regardless of our efforts to turn off the spigot and clear out the bucket of our Altered Reality, some or all of the baggage will always be left.

The technique that I use is mentally assigning my Altered Reality to something physical. For me it is a wetsuit. I envision myself taking off a wetsuit that is made up of all the limitations of my Altered Reality and placing it in a stone box with a lid that I slide into place like a stone tomb.

What is left in my mentalism is my energy body devoid of Altered Reality.

My mind is still and quiet and connected with my consciousness.

This is a mental exercise, and it takes practice and work.

Once the mind is quiet, we need to keep it quiet and there are certain biological realities about our existence in this Earth life system that help keep it quiet.

Chief among those is regulation of our vagus nerve that works as a furnace to keep Altered Reality thoughts generating as part of our biological existence.

Regulating our vagus nerve has become an industry unto itself and you can find all sorts of gadgets intended to regulate our vagus nerve sold online and in stores.

But there are simple, free and ancient ways to do this.

Many mediation practices include humming, like the sound "om."

The larynx or voice box is connected to the vagus nerve and humming while you exhale as you intentionally breathe is an excellent way to maintain stillness in your biological mind before attempting to move into the realm of the mentalism of the All.

After I have quieted my mind by placing my wetsuit in the tomb, I hum on my exhales through a breath practice until I feel my mind securely still and quiet.

These first two steps can require a significant amount of practice.

Daily practice helps build our ability to achieve these states at all, and then, additional practice allows us to achieve these states more quickly over time.

Once we have achieved a securely still and quiet mind, the third step is to separate our consciousness from our body so that we are not distracted by thoughts from the biological connection to our body.

I visualize a physical separation where the stimuli coming from my body are still there but detached and quiet, it can be helpful to imagine letting go of body parts one at a time and practicing that over time until you can release from your body in one step.

This is a critical step in releasing ourselves from the last parts of our Altered Reality.

It can be frightening to detach from your body and mind, in my experience, takes time and practice to achieve, but the result is liberating.

Separating our consciousness from our mind and body allows our consciousness to move freely anywhere or multiple places at once.

I use this time to visit people, usually hugging each of my daughters and anyone else that I believe could use a hug.

Remember that consciousness is like quantum physics and not like things we experience in our daily lives. The rules are not the same, and the Hermetic principles apply.

It takes practice to just get through those first three steps, but they are steps that Zeland ignores that I believe are fundamentally important before a deeper practice is possible.

Some may call this transurfing, but I just view it as refocusing our inner selves.

Life requires both time and space. Consciousness does not require either.

When we intentionally live in our consciousness our life becomes a series of infinite moments and we learn the blissful nature of our True Reality.

Connecting to the Intuition of Our Soul

As we previously discussed, to get to someplace thar fulfills us we need to first know where we are starting from and what fulfills us.

Mediating on who we are and what brings us bliss is a critical step to intentional manifestation.

The intuition of our soul provides many answers regarding both who we are and what fulfills us.

After we have achieved the first three steps with regularity and a level of ease, we are ready to begin to explore intuition from our soul which is the guiding force of our connection to the mentalism of the All.

It is critical to remember the Hermetic principles and know that we are not alone in the mentalism of the All. Others are there as well, and they will help us if we ask them to in our journey.

First, we must accept that we are in control of our reality. Getting in touch with our intuition is an exercise and practice in understanding the pattern of connection to our consciousness.

We have all had intuitions during our lives.

Some of these intuitions may have had significant impacts on your life decisions. Yet we have generally convinced ourselves that these intuitions are passive and happenstance.

If we focus on the pattern of those times of our strongest intuitions, we begin to find patterns that we can begin to replicate control. There is no reason not to live life in a constant state of intuition.

The power of being able to move to a state of consciousness that is expansive enough to connect with our intuition or soul at will without distraction from our Altered Reality is easier for some to do than for others.

So where do we look?

For me there are two aspects of intuition from our souls. One that I call inspiration or channeling, what some call "flow," and the other that I call forward intuition that some might call epiphany.

The difference between the two is that the first, inspiration/channeling is "real time." It is a current flow where our immediate actions are guided by our intuition.

Forward intuition, on the other hand, is a sense of flow over time where our longer-term actions are guided by our intuition.

We experience the current flow, inspiration/channeling in activities that we engage in where we interact with the energies of the universe like we do in music and sport.

An athlete may feel like she is "in the zone."

A musician can feel it when channeling a musical composition or when performing on stage.

The musical artist Maggie Rogers described it well in the title of her Harvard thesis "Surrender: Cultural Consciousness, the Spirituality of Public Gatherings."

For me, when I perform music on stage, there are nights where I find myself concentrating on the notes and chords and sounds that my part in the music requires. That is merely playing.

On other nights, and more and more nights as I put what we discuss here into practice, I pay little or no attention to the notes and chords I am playing but instead deliver energy that I feel the audience needs from my part in the music. I am playing the correct chords and notes, but if I look down at my fingers, they seem to be guiding themselves. That is channeling.

We all connect to the greater energies of the All at points in our life, sometimes through our interaction with other obvious matter in this Earth life system.

Surfers must connect to the energy of the wave.

Skiers must connect to the energy of the snow.

These interactions are magical and blissful, but they are patterns that help us understand the pattern of conscious connection to the inspiration/channeling part of intuition.

Since we have all had these experiences, we have experienced their patterns, but we spend little time intentionally exploring and practicing those patterns even if they are the most magical and blissful times in our lives.

But we can practice them.

First we explore the patterns repeatedly as part of a meditation practice. We do this by first clearing our minds and making them still and quiet as we have discussed above.

Then we think about those channeling experiences and the subtle patterns they manifest as. We begin to intentionally incorporate these patterns in our mentalism through repetitive meditation practice. We are on a pathway to reconnecting with our soul.

The connection involves a letting go that involves an opening of ourselves to receiving the patterns, and it can be fear inducing to give up the control necessary to allow ourselves to receive thoughts from our consciousness.

Letting go is a critical part of gaining control.

After we have repeatedly focused on the pattern of inspiration/ channeling we can invoke it at will even when we are not meditating because we have built a "muscle memory" of the pattern.

What I am describing is more of a practice than an achievement, at least for me. For me it requires consistent use and often the practical realities of my life get in the way and I have to go back to the meditation.

Once we have built a practice of exploring channeling, we can then move into the intentional exploration of the pattern of forward intuition.

To do this, in meditation, we focus on those experiences which were not merely channeling, but which gave us insight into the future through a knowledge of a flow over time.

For me the pattern of forward intuition is best described as a river where I can sense the start and direction of the flow of water. Friends of mine have described it as an epiphany.

Just like with channeling, with practice we can open ourselves to this conscious connection and thereby open ourselves to receiving information about these flows.

Much as our practice in channeling can allow us to channel at will without meditation, we can do the same with forward intuition with practice.

There is no reason we cannot live in a constant state of this connection, channeling, and forward intuition.

Note that the patterns and thoughts derived from our consciousness as we engage in these practices are often different in nature from those we are used to generating in our Altered Reality in that they can take any form at all.

We are so accustomed to experiencing through our senses that we are less experiences at merely experiencing.

The reward of this practice is immense, as it allows us to take control of our reality through choice by making the connection with our soul more prevalent in our lives in this Earth life system.

During all of this work and practice, our Altered Reality thoughts may tell us that what we are doing is futile or that it is all "fake" because it does not relate to our Altered Reality.

We invented the term supernatural to mean things that do not relate to or are not explainable by our Altered Reality.

We will look for ways to disprove that what we are doing is valuable, and because the All is very different than our Altered Reality, it will often present itself in supernatural ways that allow our Altered Reality to dismiss it as not real.

For example, the All and the intuition of our soul do not exist in our time and space. The results of intuitions may not be linear because the concept of linear is an Altered Reality concept.

Accordingly, there may be what appear to us as bumps in the road on our way to manifestation and creation, and those bumps can often prevent us from continuing on the path.

They act as negative bias affirmations for our negative thoughts.

Our System 1 thinking has evolved to dispense of conscious experiences that do not serve as affirmations of our experience in our Altered Reality.

Don't let it.

As Zeland suggests, at any point in your life there are an infinite number of paths to take. Our soul is what tells us the right one to take from the most efficient and effective to the least and everything in between. It is always our choice.

Regardless of our choice at any point, we have the opportunity again at each following point of our lives to choose again. But the only way to make the right or better choice that leads to our success and happiness is by consistently listening to our soul.

Our Altered Reality thoughts will play other tricks on us.

Our Altered Reality thoughts are filled with hopes, dreams, fears, and beliefs that manifest in us as a competitor to inspiration, channeling and intuition.

These are false intuitions. They sometimes feel powerful and are sometimes at odds with our soulful intuition.

We may not want to hear the intuition that our team is going to lose, when our hopeful intuition tells us they will win.

Part of the journey of moving past these false intuitions is in the practice of moving out of our Altered Reality. Many of these false intuitions derive from System 1 affirmations that we are constantly working to undo.

Everything we have discussed is aimed at freeing us from the doubts, fears and limitations and even false hopes and dreams of our Altered Reality.

Our soulful intuition is ambivalent to whether it is the intuition we want to hear.

Over time, as we shed the baggage of our Altered Reality and pay careful attention to the patterns of our intuition, we begin to understand the nature of our true soulful intuition and the false intuitions dissipate.

Chapter 14

Manifestation and Creation

Once we have reconnected with the All through our soul and the intuition it provides, we become capable of what seems like the supernatural, the creation of our own reality.

We move past our fears and limitations, and we learn new and more effective ways to manifest and create, wasting less time on fruitless activities.

I cannot emphasize enough that the transition to this can be difficult as it may become clear to us that things that we have spent significant time on will not be successful and need to be abandoned. We might lose money. We might lose relationships.

Because it is not always easy to move our lives into the direction of manifestation and creation, in our Altered Reality we will look for reasons to deny that we can manifest or create at all.

It can become easy to fall back into old Altered Reality patterns. They will feel safer to us, but they are more dangerous.

We may attempt to apply Scientific Method to our manifestation and creation, and we will fail to prove it, because, as I have discussed before, manifestation and creation are dependent on the state of the All at any point in time and that state is uncontrollable.

It is easy to tell ourselves that if something is not provable by Scientific Method it is not real. We call it supernatural.

The reality of the All, however, as we have discussed, by its nature, does not provide the controls required for the Scientific Method. The only way to know it is through our soul.

By way of example, we can't ask a skier to manifest a powder skiing day when there is no powder snow, we can't ask a surfer to manifest a great big wave ride on a flat day, and we can't ask a sailor to replicate a race on a day with no wind.

Moreover, we can't ask them to precisely manifest or create an exact replica of a ski run, a surf session or a sailing race even on the same day.

Manifestation and creation are always available to us, just in the context of the All at the point of choice.

Manifestation and creation do not occur in a vacuum, but they are not just opportunistic. Manifestation and creation are a combination of both our ability to listen and our ability to affect. They are an interaction of male and female elements operating in symphony with the nature of the All.

I find that intensity of will and desire are necessary when it comes to manifestation. Manifestation takes work. It takes committed and repetitive mentalism.

We are not just waiting for an opportunity but understanding the alignment and correspondence necessary to achieve what we want to achieve and then applying our will when our intuition reveals the path.

So how do we do it?

Close your eyes and go through the first three steps of the last Chapter clearing your mind and making it still and quiet. We are now ready.

First, we build a foundation and then we build a house on that foundation.

Try this simple exercise and appreciate that it is not all that simple.

Define the life pattern you truly want. Not one that you read about someone else having, but the life pattern that you at your truest version of you would want to lead.

What we truly want is often very hard to pull out of our Altered Reality. We have so much baggage created by Zeland pendulums, beliefs, expectations of others, life experiences that knowing what we want is complex.

Yet figuring out what we truly want is critical because it is the only way to be authentic in our manifestation and consistent with the Hermetic rules, particularly that of correspondence.

Correspondence, the idea of "as above, so below," means that we have to be consistent on all levels of our existence in order to manifest and create. Taking control of our reality requires correspondence.

When we believe we have an idea of our true self, we think of what that means to us in terms of your physical, mental, emotional and even divine self and what we want to accomplish in that life pattern.

Close your eyes, use the practice we have discussed to clear your mind of Altered Reality and while engaging in a breathing practice use your mind to manifest each of these things in your mentalism one by one.

To start, create a pattern of your physical self that reflects your true desire of how you want to be physically. Intensely and intentionally focus on that physical pattern so it is the only thing in your mentalism and then deliver that pattern into your consciousness to hand it off to your soul to release it into the All.

It is now part of the mentalism of the All and it becomes more and more pure with practice both externally and internally.

Without this exercise we are likely sending multiple realities into the All that may conflict reflecting conflicting messages within ourselves.

Perform this same practice with each aspect of your life. Follow the physical pattern with the mental pattern, then the emotional pattern and then the pattern of what you want to accomplish.

It may take many times of practice to finally gain a clear vision of these patterns, and as we practice, we are accomplishing two things.

First, we begin to define our true selves clearly to ourselves.

Second, we are inserting the mentalism of our true selves vividly into the mentalism of the All. We thereby create a powerful and pure correspondence.

This correspondence is the foundation of manifestation because without defining the foundation of our true selves we cannot build the house of manifestation and creation above it.

We all want things to come as easily as possible. We want to cure a cold with a pill, sleeplessness with a pill, anxiety with a pill.

Similarly, we may want to believe that we can manifest things merely by writing them down or pretending some goal is our reality.

But manifestation is hard work and it takes repetitively ensuring that the foundation is sound and true both internally and externally, and then manifesting and creating the house above it using information about the All that only our soul can provide.

We need to manifest and create on all planes of existence, and it requires our complete dedication on every plane.

On every plane we will have choices.

Therefore, once we have built our own pattern and repeatedly delivered it to the All, we are then ready to use the intuition provided by our soul to guide us to make choices consistent with the pattern we have built.

This takes practice as well.

The intuition of our soul at every point of our life allows us to make choices consistent with both our true nature and the nature of the All.

It takes into consideration the rules of the All: mentalism, correspondence, vibration, polarity, rhythm, cause and effect and gender.

Some of these are like weather conditions: vibration, polarity, rhythm that require our soul to act like a meteorologist for us.

Others like cause and effect and gender are things that we need to understand in order to manifest and create.

When we need to cause something or someone to do something, we must understand how to use the male to cause the female to act. We need to understand the cause and effect of that action and whether it is possible given the conditions present.

All creation comes from the male and female principle of Hermetics, in the context and pattern of the other principles.

The male energy triggers the female energy to create, but the female energy must be open to that creation. Intuition guides us in knowing when and where that is the case.

Understanding what the female and male elements are during manifestation and creation is critical as they always exist. It is, therefore, important to know what entices the female element to produce before creating.

Understanding that the female and male do not exist in a vacuum but rather in the other Hermetic rules is also critical, and the alignment of those rules can be felt through intuition.

I once took a friend skiing on a snowy day with low visability. He was an advanced intermediate, near expert skier who had limited experience skiing powder snow.

The snow was deep and light that day, but it was hard to see.

I told him that skiing powder snow was different than skiing groomed snow because you needed to listen more to the snow before you chose how to act.

The balance between the male (body decision) and female (snow reality) was different. Manifesting a great ski run required much more release to the information provided by the snow, the male listening more to the female.

He skied amazingly that day. Flowing gracefully though beautiful arcing curves in the deep white powder.

He benefited from not having the sense of vision which would have interrupted his communication with the snow with limiting thoughts of fear and survival.

He was in complete conformity with all the Hermetic principles, most importantly that of gender.

The next day the sun came out. A beautiful blue sky against the white mountains.

I took him to the same ski run and he kept falling.

His ability to see the snow had created thoughts of fear and doubt. He had lost his connection to the All. His male element was not listening to the female element. He was out of correspondence and out of touch with the other Hermetic principles.

Without listening to our soul, even if we have created the pattern of our true selves, we are a ship without a captain at sea.

Little if anything of what I have told you here has affirmation in our Altered Reality, and it requires a significant amount of constant work and maybe even "faith."

Do not let your Altered Reality thoughts dissuade you from the practice because they will try and convince you that it is not real.

In fact, the practice leads you to the only reality, and it will seem supernatural when you not only realize that your reality is entirely in your own hands but that you can manifest and create things you never believed possible when you have achieved the pure correspondence and a connection to the All through your soul.

Our consciousness is always magical and even more so when we expand it into the infinity of the All.

Chapter 15

The Gateway Experience: Hemi-sync Meditation

I want to conclude Part 2 by offering some insights into meditation that I have found particularly valuable in finding my way to taking control of my reality.

Vadim Zeland and others will tell you that you do not need meditation or hard work.

Possibly you don't.

I do.

I discovered The Gateway Experience in 2023 and have been regularly meditating using it every day.

Robert Monroe was a radio executive who produced quiz shows and other programs for popular radio. In the late 1950s and early 1960s, Monroe began using sound waves to cause Frequency Following Response in human brains.

Frequency Following Response, or FFR is a condition where brain waves are stimulated to replicate the frequency of the sound waves.

Earlier in this book we discussed the Schumann Resonance and how it relates to human Alpha waves. The background Schumann Resonance could be the FFR source of Alpha waves.

Monroe found that he could manipulate brain waves into nearly any relaxation state. In particular, Monroe found that he could induce sleep cycles using this methodology.

As research progressed, Monroe and his team discovered that by providing different sound patterns to each ear, they could synchronize brain waves in each hemisphere. The name hemi-sync was coined.

In hemi-sync meditation, "phased sine waves at discernible sound frequencies, are blended to create binaural "beat" frequencies within the ranges or electrical brain waves found at the various stages of human sleep, create a Frequency Following Response (FFR) within the EEG pattern of the individual listening to such audio wave forms." Monroe Institute "Early History and Research Article".

Monroe and his team found that they could use binaural (two ear) stimulation to: (1) balance health, (2) reduce stress, (3) surgical support, (4) pain control, (5) stroke recovery, (6) psychotherapy, (7) problem solving, and (8) accelerated learning.

All these things seem supernatural. They are not. They are all within our ability through our taking control of our reality through our consciousness, our soul and our connection to the All.

Of importance to this book, Monroe and his team found that hemi-sync training could be used to dramatically strengthen meditation practice to, among other things, remote view, develop intuitive skills, manifest and create, move around planes of existence, discover the life and energy forces associated with your soul, even talk to the dead.

The meditation practice is performed at your own pace, and you work through a number of exercises intended to build your ability to move into different meditative states and planes of existence called "focuses."

Whether this meditation appeals to you or not, it is the basis of significant research by the Central Intelligence Agency and U.S. Army Intelligence.

Now public, a report released in 2003 but written in 1983 demonstrates that the U.S. Army and Central Intelligence Agency had been studying the ways that hemi-sync training systems can enhance "the strength, focus and coherence... of brainwave output between the left and right hemispheres so as to alter consciousness, moving it outside the physical sphere so as to ultimately escape even the restrictions of time and space." Department of the Army CIA-RDP96-00788R001700210016-5.

It has been reported and documented that using hemi-sync meditation some have achieved levels of very precise remote visualization.

Joseph McMoneagle is one of those who went through the military remote viewing program and claims to have among other things remotely described the location and general description of the top secret Russian Typhoon Class submarine, determined the location of a captured US Army general and determined the location of a crashed Soviet bomber. See *Mind Trek: Exploring Consciousness, Time, and Space Through Remote Viewing*. Hampton Roads Publishing Company. 1993.

Others have reported sensing tragic events, manifesting outcomes and reading minds.

My own personal journey with the meditation started with a simple need to lose the fears and limitations that were holding me back as a business leader and to relieve stress.

As I moved into deeper "focuses," I found myself exploring my own limiting thoughts and beliefs and my own journey beyond just the journey in this life in this Earth life system.

Relatively early on, I moved into focuses that I can only describe as near death where I found great comfort in experiencing that death is immensely blissful, almost choosing not to return from my meditative state, and when I did, I found that I was not breathing, and it took great effort to refill my lungs.

During those early sessions, I experienced a blow to my ribs and witnessed a friend who I will call John laying on the ground on his right side, unable to roll to his left side because of the pain.

Worried that John might have had a heart attack, I had my wife contact John who was more her friend than mine to ask if he was okay and he reported that he had taken a blow to the ribs and had broken several of them and could not lay on his left side.

I was not seeking that kind of validation, but it led to very intense meditations around manifestation and intuition that led to, among other things, the need to write this book.

I journeyed through past lives and my existence before this life.

I found an inner spirit, another soul, that is female that has been bonded to me through many existences. I still have much to learn and visit often.

I still wonder why I came back to this Earth life system this time.

My Altered Reality thoughts continue to create limitations for me.

Like I have said, it is a practice, and we can only strive to keep moving in the right direction.

I find great comfort daily moving to other planes of existence that are more natural and common to me than life in this Earth life system.

What I find appealing about this meditation is that it predates and is consistent with Orch OR theories and is very aligned with Hermetic principles.

Hemi-sync meditation is a long practice that requires mastering certain skills before moving to the next level. It is done at your own pace.

In my practical reality, the meditation has helped me find clarity and purpose, break away from self-destructive and wasteful habits resulting in a streamlining of businesses and a much clearer focus on business opportunities.

Each meditation is a practice leading to my understanding that my reality is in my control, that I am magical, and that a connection with my soul and with the All and all the clarity and unlimited possibility that the connection permits is my path to blissful existence in this Earth life system.

Now it is up to you. I have given you everything that you need.

Bibliography

The Three Initiates. (1908). *The Kybalion: A Study of the Hermetic Philosophy of Ancient Egypt and Greece*. Chicago. Yogi Publication Society.

Randall, Lisa. (2015). *Dark Matter and the Dinosaurs: The Astounding Interconnectedness of the Universe*. New York. Harper Collins.

Randall, Lisa. (2005). *Warped Passages: Unraveling the Mysteries of the Universe's Hidden Dimensions*. New York. Harper Collins.

Kahneman, Daniel. (2013). *Thinking, Fast and Slow*. New York. Farrar, Strauss and Giroux.

Firstenberg, Arthur. (2017). *The Invisible Rainbow: A History of Electricity and Life*. Washington, D.C., AGB Press.

Mayer, Emeran. (2106). *Mind-Gut Connection*. New York. Harper Collins.

Shah, Amy. (2021) *I'm So Effing Tired: A Proven Plan to Beat Burnout, Boost Your Energy, and Reclaim Your Life*. London. Little Brown Book Group.

Bernays, Edward. (1928). *Propaganda*. New York. Horace Liveright, Inc.

Bernays, Edward. (1923). *Crystalizing Public Opinion*. New York. Horace Liveright, Inc.

Gurri, Martin. (2018). *The Revolt of the Public and the Crisis of Authority in the New Millennium*. San Francisco. Stripe Book Press.

Bernstein, Andrew. (2015). *The Myth of Stress*. New York. Atria.

Zeland, Vadim. (2008). *Transurfing of Reality*. London. O-Books.

McMoneagle, Joseph. (1993) *Mind Trek: Exploring Consciousness, Time, and Space Through Remote Viewing*. Newburyport, MA. Hampton Roads Publishing Company.

Don't miss out!

Visit the website below and you can sign up to receive emails whenever Derek Pew publishes a new book. There's no charge and no obligation.

https://books2read.com/r/B-A-VZUEC-CRDNE

BOOKS 2 READ

Connecting independent readers to independent writers.

About the Author

Derek Pew, age 58.

Derek is a thought leader in the world of digital currencies. An accomplished investment banker and securities lawyer, Derek became a serial social entrepreneur in 1998 building companies in the areas of wireless access to provide digital divide solutions, cultural performing arts digital distribution, youth development through video gaming, and is currently focused on global uses of digital currencies.

Working on cutting edge solutions and building and managing companies in those spaces, Derek became aware of a number of personal traits that were limiting his effectiveness as a business leader and sought out a CEO coach that led him to a meditation practice used by the Central Intelligence Agency.

Derek used that practice to identify and reduce the impact of self-imposed limitations, and work towards existing in an intuitive state that supported effective manifestation and creation in his work and personal life. Without any intention to write a book, the significant realizations that came from this practice flowed out of Derek like a song in the form of the manuscript he is submitting. Derek believes that everyone should read what he has written because it will give them a better perspective reality that allows them to live a more complete life.

A graduate of Dartmouth College with honors in Economics, and a graduate of The Law School of the University of Pennsylvania, Derek has served on numerous charitable boards including: MANNA, The Greene Town School, The Agnes Irwin School, The Free Library of Philadelphia Foundation, The Philadelphia Orchestra, and The Law School of the University of Pennsylvania.

When not working, Derek spends his time with his wife and two adult daughters, travels, plays in two rock bands, surfs, plays squash and tennis, skis and attempts to resurrect his golf game.

Read more at https://derek-pew.com.